THE 2,320 FUNNIEST Quotes

THE

Most Hilaricus

Quips and One-Liners from

ALLGREATQUOTES.COM

COMPILED BY TOM CORR

Ulysses Press

Concept and Compilation © 2011 Tom Corr.

Published in the United States by
ULYSSES PRESS
P.O. Box 3440
Berkeley, CA 94703
www.ulyssespress.com

ISBN: 978-1-56975-975-2
Library of Congress Catalog Number 2011926013

Acquisitions Editor: Kelly Reed
Managing Editor: Claire Chun
Editor: Sayre Van Young
Proofreaders: Lauren Harrison, Lee Micheaux
Production: Judith Metzener
Front cover design: what!design @ whatweb.com

Printed in the United States by Bang Printing

10 9 8 7 6 5 4 3 2 1

Distributed by Publishers Group West

Contents

Actors, Hollywood, and the Movies

Half the people in Hollywood are dying to be discovered and the other half are afraid they will be.
— *Lionel Barrymore*

Hollywood is where they shoot too many pictures and not enough actors.
— *Walter Winchell*

There are only three ages for women in Hollywood—Babe, District Attorney, and Driving Miss Daisy.
— *Goldie Hawn, in* The First Wives Club

Hollywood is a place where they'll pay you a thousand dollars for a kiss and fifty cents for your soul.
— *Marilyn Monroe*

There are five stages in the life of an actor: Who's Mary Astor? Get me Mary Astor. Get me a Mary Astor Type. Get me a young Mary Astor. Who's Mary Astor?
— *Mary Astor*

Show business is dog-eat-dog. It's worse than dog-eat-dog, it's-dog-doesn't-return-other-dog's-phone-calls.
> —*Woody Allen,* Crimes and Misdemeanors

I love acting. It is so much more real than life.
> —*Oscar Wilde,* The Picture of Dorian Gray

We're actors—we're the opposite of people.
> —*Tom Stoppard,*
> Rosencrantz and Guildenstern Are Dead

Acting is all about honesty. If you can fake that, you've got it made.
> —*George Burns*

I'm not a real movie star. I've still got the same wife I started out with 28 years ago.
> —*Will Rogers*

In Westerns, you were permitted to kiss your horse but never your girl.
> —*Gary Cooper*

In Hollywood, brides keep the bouquets and throw away
the groom.
— *Groucho Marx*

In Hollywood now when people die they don't say, "Did he
leave a will?" but "Did he leave a diary?"
— *Liza Minnelli*

An actor's a guy who, if you ain't talking about him,
ain't listening.
— *Marlon Brando*

When you're called a character actress it's because you are
too ugly to be called a leading lady.
— *Kathy Burke*

We're overpaying him, but he's worth it.
— *Samuel Goldwyn*

You don't need to retire as an actor, there are all those parts
you can play lying in bed, or in a wheelchair.
— *Judi Dench*

Show me a great actor and I'll show you a lousy husband.
Show me a great actress, and you've seen the devil.
　　—*W. C. Fields*

We in the industry know that behind every successful
screenwriter stands a woman. And behind her stands
his wife.
　　—*Groucho Marx*

People tell me that the movies should be more like real life.
I disagree. It is real life that should be more like the movies.
　　—*Walter Winchell*

Hollywood is the only place where you can wake up in the
morning and hear the birds coughing in the trees.
　　—*Joe Frisco*

Hollywood is an asylum run by the inmates.
　　—*Laurence Stallings*

People find out I'm an actress and I see that "whore" look
flicker across their eyes.
　　—*Rachel Weisz*

When an actor marries an actress they both fight for the mirror.
—*Burt Reynolds*

The reason why so many people showed up at his [Louis B. Mayer's] funeral was because they wanted to make sure he was dead.
—*Samuel Goldwyn*

Giving your book to Hollywood is like turning your daughter over to a pimp.
—*Tom Clancy*

Never let that son of a bitch in the studio again— until we need him.
—*Samuel Goldwyn*

Working in Hollywood does give one a certain expertise in the field of prostitution.
—*Jane Fonda*

Hollywood is a trip through a sewer in a glass-bottomed boat.
—*Wilson Mizner*

The world is a stage, but the play is badly cast.
— *Oscar Wilde,* Lord Arthur Savile's Crime

If I made *Cinderella*, the audience would immediately be looking for a body in the coach.
— *Alfred Hitchcock*

After *The Wizard of Oz* I was typecast as a lion, and there aren't all that many parts for lions.
— *Bert Lahr*

I don't want any yes-men around me. I want everyone to tell me the truth even if it costs them their jobs.
— *Samuel Goldwyn*

Age, Old Age, and Youth

Youth is wasted on the young.
— *George Bernard Shaw*

Youth would be an ideal state if it came a little later in life.
— *Herbert Asquith*

Age, Old Age, and Youth

I recently turned 60. Practically a third of my life is over.
  — *Woody Allen*

Life begins at 40—but so do fallen arches, rheumatism, faulty eyesight, and the tendency to tell a story to the same person three or four times.
  — *Helen Rowland*

Old age isn't so bad when you consider the alternative.
  — *Maurice Chevalier*

Old age is no place for sissies.
  — *Bette Davis [among many others, including H. L. Mencken and Art Linkletter]*

People ask me what I'd most appreciate getting for my eighty-seventh birthday. I tell them: a paternity suit.
  — *George Burns*

There's one more terrifying fact about old people: I'm going to be one soon.
  — *P. J. O'Rourke*

You can live to be a 100 if you give up all the things that make you want to live to be a 100.
— *Woody Allen*

I'm 74 years old and even though I may be a bit of a rascal… 33 girls in two months seems to me too much even for a 30-year-old.
— *Silvio Berlusconi, Italian prime minister, on vice allegations*

The old believe everything, the middle-aged suspect everything, the young know everything.
— *Oscar Wilde*

The hardest years in life are those between 10 and 70.
— *Helen Hayes, at 73*

The three ages of man: youth, middle age, and "my word you do look well."
— *June Whitfield*

Old age is like a plane flying through a storm. Once you're aboard, there's nothing you can do about it.
— *Golda Meir*

You want to look younger? Rent smaller children.
— *Phyllis Diller*

Thirty-five is a very attractive age. London society is full of women of the very highest birth who have, of their own free choice, remained 35 for years.
— *Oscar Wilde,* The Importance of Being Earnest

At 20 years of age, the will reigns; at 30, the wit; and at 40, the judgment.
— *Benjamin Franklin,* Poor Richard's Almanack

Youth is something very new: 20 years ago no one mentioned it.
— *Coco Chanel*

To me, old age is always 15 years older than I am.
— *Bernard Baruch*

Allow me to put the record straight. I am 46 and have been for some years past.
— *Erica Jong*

Youth is a disease from which we all recover.
— *Dorothy Fuldheim*

At my age, flowers scare me.
— *George Burns*

I don't know how you feel about old age, but in my case I didn't see it coming. It hit me in the rear.
— *Phyllis Diller*

You're never too old to become younger.
— *Mae West*

One should never trust a woman who tells one her real age. A woman who would tell one that, would tell one anything.
— *Oscar Wilde,* A Woman of No Importance

There are no old people nowadays; they are either "wonderful for their age" or dead.
— *Mary Pettibone Poole*

It is sad to grow old but nice to ripen.
— *Brigitte Bardot*

Age, Old Age, and Youth

I don't feel old—I don't feel anything until noon. Then it's
time for my nap.
> —*Bob Hope*

You know you're old if they have discontinued your
blood type.
> —*Phyllis Diller*

I still think of myself as I was 25 years ago. Then I look in a
mirror and see an old bastard and realize it's me.
> —*Dave Allen*

Youth, which is forgiven everything, forgives itself nothing;
age, which forgives itself everything, is forgiven nothing.
> —*George Bernard Shaw,* Man and Superman

As I grow older and older
And totter toward the tomb
I find that I care less and less
Who goes to bed with whom.
> —*Dorothy L. Sayers*

When the age is in, the wit is out.
> —*William Shakespeare,* Much Ado About Nothing

My mother always used to say, "The older you get, the better you get, unless you're a banana."
  — *Betty White as Rose Nylund, on* The Golden Girls

Age to women is like Kryptonite to Superman.
  — *Kathy Lette*

I'm at that age now where just putting my cigar in its holder is a thrill.
  — *George Burns*

No woman should ever be quite accurate about her age. It looks so calculating.
  — *Oscar Wilde,* The Importance of Being Earnest

Every man over 40 is a scoundrel.
  — *George Bernard Shaw,* Man and Superman

Age is not a particularly interesting subject. Anyone can get old. All you have to do is live long enough.
  — *Groucho Marx*

When I was a boy of 14, my father was so ignorant I could hardly stand to have the old man around. But when I got to be 21, I was astonished at how much the old man had learned in seven years.
    —*Mark Twain, attributed*

Women are as old as they feel—and men are old when they lose their feelings.
    —*Mae West*

I delight in men over 70. They always offer one the devotion of a lifetime. I think 70 an ideal age for a man.
    —*Oscar Wilde,* A Woman of No Importance

Age is something that doesn't matter, unless you are a cheese.
    —*Billie Burke*

To get back my youth I would do anything in the world, except take exercise, get up early, or be respectable.
    —*Oscar Wilde,* The Picture of Dorian Gray

Alcohol and Other Drugs

There can't be good living where there is not good drinking.
—*Benjamin Franklin*

Life is good, but wine is better.
—*Fernando Pessoa*

Pour him out of here!
—*Mae West, on W. C. Fields arriving drunk on a movie set*

Work is the curse of the drinking classes.
—*Oscar Wilde*

I drink, therefore I am.
—*W. C. Fields*

I feel sorry for people who don't drink. They wake up in the morning, that's as good as they're going to feel all day.
—*Frank Sinatra [among others, including Dean Martin]*

Now son, you don't want to drink beer. That's for daddies, and kids with fake IDs.
—*Homer Simpson, on* The Simpsons

Cocaine habit-forming? Of course not. I ought to know. I've been using it for years.
—*Tallulah Bankhead*

In 1969 I gave up women and alcohol. It was the worst 20 minutes of my life.
—*George Best*

I'm only a beer teetotaler, not a champagne teetotaler.
—*George Bernard Shaw,* Candida

Only Irish coffee provides in a single glass all four essential food groups: alcohol, caffeine, sugar, and fat.
—*Alex Levine*

I like my whiskey old and my women young.
—*Errol Flynn*

Drink, sir, is a great provoker of three things...nose-painting, sleep, and urine. Lechery, sir, it provokes, and unprovokes; it provokes the desire, but it takes away the performance....
— *William Shakespeare,* Macbeth

You find out so many interesting things when you're not on drugs.
— *Boy George*

If you drink, don't drive. Don't even putt.
— *Dean Martin*

I am not a heavy drinker. I can sometimes go for hours without touching a drop.
— *Noël Coward*

When money's tight and is hard to get
And your horse has also ran,
When all you have is a heap of debt—
A PINT OF PLAIN IS YOUR ONLY MAN.
— *Flann O'Brien,* At Swim-Two-Birds

I only take a drink on two occasions—when I'm thirsty and when I'm not.
— *Brendan Behan*

I have made an important discovery—that alcohol, taken in sufficient quantities, produces all the effects of intoxication.
    —Oscar Wilde

It takes only one drink to get me drunk. The trouble is, I can't remember if it's the thirteenth or the fourteenth.
    —George Burns

I believe a lot of you are into gardening—security officers said you were growing your own grass.
    —Bob Hope, on tour of troops in Vietnam

You're not drunk if you can lie on the floor without holding on.
    —Dean Martin

Cocaine is God's way of saying you're making too much money.
    —Robin Williams

My dad was the town drunk. Most of the time that's not so bad—but New York City?
    —Henny Youngman

Whiskey is by far the most popular of all remedies that won't cure a cold.
> —*Jerry Vale*

What contemptible scoundrel stole the cork from my lunch?
> —*W. C. Fields*

Candy
Is dandy
But liquor
Is quicker.
> —*Ogden Nash*

When I read about the evils of drinking, I gave up reading.
> —*Henny Youngman*

The last mosquito that bit me had to check into the Betty Ford clinic.
> —*Joanna Lumley as Patsy Stone,*
> *on* Absolutely Fabulous

I know I'm drinking myself to a slow death, but then I'm in no hurry.
> —*Robert Benchley*

Love makes the world go round? Not at all. Whisky makes it go round twice as fast.
— *Compton Mackenzie,* Whisky Galore

Not one man in a beer commercial has a beer belly.
— *Rita Rudner*

The difference between a drunk and an alcoholic is that a drunk doesn't have to attend all those meetings.
— *Arthur Lewis*

The AAAA is a new organization for drunks who drive. Give them a call and they'll tow you away from the bar.
— *Martin Burden*

I'd stay away from Ecstasy. This is a drug so strong it makes white people think they can dance.
— *Lenny Henry*

His mouth had been used as a latrine by some small creature of the night, and then as its mausoleum.
— *Kingsley Amis, describing a hangover in* Lucky Jim

For a bad hangover take the juice of two quarts of whiskey.
— *Eddie Condon*

One tequila, two tequila, three tequila, floor.
— *George Carlin*

I have taken more out of alcohol than alcohol has taken out of me.
— *Winston Churchill*

They're trying to put warning labels on liquor saying, "Caution, alcohol can be dangerous to pregnant women." That's ironic. If it weren't for alcohol, most women wouldn't even be that way.
— *Rita Rudner*

I am a drinker with writing problems.
— *Brendan Behan*

Never take Ecstasy, beer, Bacardi, weed, Pepto Bismol, Vivarin, Tums, Tagamet HB, Xanax, and Valium in the same day. It makes it difficult to sleep at night.
— *Eminem*

Beer. Helping Ugly People Have Sex Since 1862.
   — T-shirt slogan

I spent a lot of my money on booze, birds, and fast cars.
The rest I just squandered.
   — George Best

I saw a notice which said "Drink Canada Dry" and I've
just started.
   — Brendan Behan

Two guys walk into a bar. You'd think one of them would
have seen it.
   — Daniel Lybra

I never drink anything stronger than gin before breakfast.
   — W. C. Fields

I don't drink liquor. I don't like it. It makes me feel good.
   — Oscar Levant

I'll die young, but it's like kissing God.
   — Lenny Bruce, on his drug addiction

Reality is just a crutch for people who can't cope with drugs.
—*Lily Tomlin*

There is nothing wrong with sobriety in moderation.
—*John Ciardi*

Drugs have taught an entire generation of American kids the metric system.
—*P. J. O'Rourke*

One reason I don't drink is that I want to know when I'm having a good time.
—*Nancy Astor*

Hi kids…don't buy drugs. Become a pop star and they give you them for free.
—*Bill Nighy as Billy Mack, in* Love Actually

I'm Bender, baby! Please insert liquor!
—*Bender [the robot], on* Futurama

Alcohol is like love: the first kiss is magic, the second is intimate, the third is routine. After that, you just take the girl's clothes off.
—*Raymond Chandler,* The Long Goodbye

A tavern is a place where madness is sold by the bottle.
—*Jonathan Swift*

The wine tasted like a urine sample from someone who is gravely ill.
—*Frank Muir*

The only cure for a real hangover is death.
—*Robert Benchley*

My grandmother is over 80 and still doesn't need glasses. Drinks right out of the bottle.
—*Henny Youngman*

Gin was mother's milk to her.
—*George Bernard Shaw,* Pygmalion

There comes a time in every woman's life when the only
thing that helps is a glass of champagne.
 —*Bette Davis, in* Old Acquaintance

There are better things in life than alcohol, but alcohol
makes up for not having them.
 —*Terry Pratchett*

Hangover: The wrath of grapes.
 —*Dorothy Parker [among others, including
 Oscar Levant and Robert Benchley]*

A bottle of wine contains more philosophy than all the books
in the world.
 —*Louis Pasteur*

An alcoholic is someone you don't like who drinks as much
as you do.
 —*Dylan Thomas*

I was so jazzed about sobering up and starting a new life, I
had to stop at a bar to get a drink just to calm down.
 —*Kristin Chenoweth as April Rhodes, on* Glee

I'll stick with gin. Champagne is just ginger ale that knows somebody.
>—*Alan Alda as Hawkeye, on* M*A*S*H

I never turned to drink. It seemed to turn to me.
>—*Brendan Behan*

Abstainer, n. A weak person who yields to the temptation of denying himself a pleasure.
>—*Ambrose Bierce,* The Devil's Dictionary

Alcohol may be man's worst enemy, but the Bible says love your enemy.
>—*Frank Sinatra*

When the wine is in, the wit is out.
>—*English proverb*

A man hath no better thing under the sun, than to eat, and to drink, and to be merry.
>—*Bible,* Ecclesiastes 8:15

Brandy, n.: A cordial composed of one part thunder-and-lightning, one part remorse, two parts bloody murder, one part death-hell-and-the-grave, and four parts clarified Satan.
   —*Ambrose Bierce,* The Devil's Dictionary

Drunkenness is simply voluntary insanity.
   —*Seneca*

Quickly, bring me a beaker of wine, so that I may wet my mind and say something clever.
   —*Aristophanes*

Without question, the greatest invention in the history of mankind is beer. Oh, I grant you that the wheel was also a fine invention, but the wheel does not go nearly as well with pizza.
   —*Dave Barry*

The problem with some people is that when they aren't drunk, they're sober.
   —*William Butler Yeats*

I like to have a martini,
Two at the very most.
After three I'm under the table,
After four I'm under my host.
>   —*Dorothy Parker*

The problem with the world is that everyone is a few
drinks behind.
>   —*Humphrey Bogart*

But I'm not so think as you drunk I am.
>   —*J. C. Squire*

No animal ever invented anything so bad as drunkenness—
or so good as drink.
>   —*G. K. Chesterton*

Even though a number of people have tried, no one has yet
found a way to drink for a living.
>   —*Jean Kerr*

America and Americans

If you don't like your job, you don't strike. You just go in every day, and do it really half-assed. That's the American way.
— *Homer Simpson, on* The Simpsons

Americans can eat garbage, provided you sprinkle it liberally with ketchup, mustard, chili sauce, Tabasco sauce, cayenne pepper, or any other condiment which destroys the original flavor of the dish.
— *Henry Miller*

America is the land of permanent waves and impermanent wives.
— *Brendan Behan*

America is a large, friendly dog in a very small room. Every time it wags its tail, it knocks over a chair.
— *Arnold Toynbee*

Americans like fat books and thin women.
— *Russell Baker*

American women expect to find in their husbands a perfection that English women only hope to find in their butlers.
— *W. Somerset Maugham*

It was wonderful to find America, but it would have been more wonderful to miss it.
— *Mark Twain*, Pudd'nhead Wilson

Americans will always do the right thing, after they've exhausted all the alternatives.
— *Winston Churchill*

I am willing to love all mankind, except an American.
— *Samuel Johnson*

America had often been discovered before Columbus, but it had always been hushed up.
— *Oscar Wilde*

America's health care system is second only to Japan, Canada, Sweden, Great Britain, well…all of Europe. But you can thank your lucky stars we don't live in Paraguay!
— *Homer Simpson, on* The Simpsons

That joke was lost on the foreigner—guides cannot master the subtleties of the American joke.
> —*Mark Twain,* The Innocents Abroad

I'm from England, the country that used to own you people.
> —*Jane Leeves as Daphne Moon, on* Frasier

She behaves as if she was beautiful. Most American women do. It is the secret of their charm.
> —*Oscar Wilde,* The Picture of Dorian Gray

An asylum for the sane would be empty in America.
> —*George Bernard Shaw*

America is becoming so educated that ignorance will be a novelty. I will belong to the select few.
> —*Will Rogers*

All Americans lecture, I believe. I suppose it is something in their climate.
> —*Oscar Wilde,* A Woman of No Importance

Never criticize Americans. They have the best taste that
money can buy.
　　　—Miles Kington

America is the only nation in history which, miraculously,
has gone directly from barbarism to degeneration without
the usual interval of civilization.
　　　—Georges Clemenceau

I don't believe there's any problem in this country, no matter
how tough it is, that Americans, when they roll up their
sleeves, can't completely ignore.
　　　—George Carlin, Brain Droppings

In America, the young are always ready to give to
those who are older than themselves the full benefits of
their inexperience.
　　　—Oscar Wilde

Half of the American people have never read a
newspaper. Half never voted for president. One hopes it is
the same half.
　　　—Gore Vidal

Frustrate a Frenchman, he will drink himself to death; an Irishman, he will die of angry hypertension; a Dane, he will shoot himself; an American, he will get drunk, shoot you, then establish a million-dollar aid program for your relatives. Then he will die of an ulcer.
— *Stanley Rudin*

Americans adore me and will go on adoring me until I say something nice about them.
— *George Bernard Shaw, attributed*

America is the only country where a significant proportion of the population believes that professional wrestling is real but the moon landing was faked.
— *David Letterman*

Ninety-eight percent of the adults in this country are decent, hard-working, honest Americans. It's the other lousy two percent that get all the publicity. But then— we elected them.
— *Lily Tomlin*

No one ever went broke underestimating the intelligence of the American people.
— *H. L. Mencken, attributed*

The American man marries early, and the American woman marries often; and they get on extremely well together.
— *Oscar Wilde*

The thing that impresses me most about America is the way parents obey their children.
— *Edward, Duke of Windsor*

America makes prodigious mistakes, America has colossal faults, but one thing cannot be denied: America is always on the move. She may be going to hell, of course, but at least she isn't standing still.
— *e. e. cummings*

America is a mistake, a giant mistake.
— *Sigmund Freud*

America is the best half-educated country in the world.
— *Nicholas Murray Butler*

Americans will put up with anything provided it doesn't block traffic.
— *Dan Rather*

Americans are people who laugh at African witch doctors and spend 100 million dollars on fake reducing systems.
—*L. L. Levinson*

We have really everything in common with America nowadays, except, of course, language.
—*Oscar Wilde,* The Canterville Ghost

Illegal aliens have always been a problem in the United States. Ask any Indian.
—*Robert Orben*

The Americans are certainly great hero-worshipers, and always take heroes from the criminal classes.
—*Oscar Wilde*

Americans are broad-minded people. They'll accept the fact that a person can be an alcoholic, a dope fiend, a wife beater, and even a newspaperman, but if a man doesn't drive, there is something wrong with him.
—*Art Buchwald*

Animals

Some of my best leading men have been dogs and horses.
  — *Elizabeth Taylor*

Our most perfect companions never have fewer than
four feet.
  — *Sidonie-Gabrielle Colette*

This is really a lovely horse. I once rode her mother.
  — *Ted Walsh, racing commentator*

Biologically speaking, if something bites you, it is more likely
to be female.
  — *Desmond Morris*

You can say any foolish thing to a dog, and the dog will give
you a look that says, "My God, you're right! I never would've
thought of that!"
  — *Dave Barry*

Getting a dog is like getting married. It teaches you to be less self-centered, to accept sudden, surprising outbursts of affection, and not to be upset by a few scratches on your car.
—*Will Stanton*

I am fond of pigs. Dogs look up to us. Cats look down on us. Pigs treat us as equals.
—*Winston Churchill, attributed*

Whenever you observe an animal closely, you feel as if a human being sitting inside were making fun of you.
—*Elias Canetti*

I believe that our Heavenly Father invented man because he was disappointed in the monkey.
—*Mark Twain*

Eagles may soar, but weasels don't get sucked into jet engines.
—*John Benfield*

I am not a vegetarian because I love animals; I am a vegetarian because I hate plants.
—*A. Whitney Brown*

Animals

My favorite animal is steak.
— *Fran Lebowitz*

I ask people why they have deer heads on their walls.
They always say because it's such a beautiful animal.
There you go. I think my mother is attractive, but I have
photographs of her.
— *Ellen DeGeneres*

To my mind, the only possible pet is a cow. Cows love you...
They will listen to your problems and never ask a thing in
return. They will be your friends forever. And when you get
tired of them, you can kill and eat them.
— *Bill Bryson*

It is inexcusable for scientists to torture animals; let them
make their experiments on journalists and politicians.
— *Henrik Ibsen*

A lady came up to me on the street and pointed at my suede
jacket. "You know a cow was murdered for that jacket?" she
sneered. I replied in a psychotic tone, "I didn't know there
were any witnesses. Now I'll have to kill you, too."
— *Jake Johannsen*

You're a good example of why some animals eat their young.
—*Jim Samuels*

There is an eagle in me that wants to soar, and there is a hippopotamus in me that wants to wallow in the mud.
—*Carl Sandburg*

Animals are my friends, and I don't eat my friends.
—*George Bernard Shaw*

Man is the only animal that blushes. Or needs to.
—*Mark Twain,* Following the Equator

The thing that differentiates man from animals is money.
—*Gertrude Stein*

It is hard to be brave, when you're only a Very Small Animal.
—*Piglet, in* Winnie-the-Pooh *by A. A. Milne*

Cat, n. A soft, indestructible automaton provided by nature to be kicked when things go wrong in the domestic circle.
—*Ambrose Bierce,* The Devil's Dictionary

Animals

To his dog, every man is Napoleon; hence the constant
popularity of dogs.
—*Aldous Huxley*

People that hate cats will come back as mice in their
next life.
—*Faith Resnick*

If you want a friend in Washington, get a dog.
—*Harry S. Truman, attributed*

A man is like a cat; chase him and he'll run; sit still and
ignore him and he'll come purring at your feet.
—*Helen Rowland*

A dog is the only thing on earth that loves you more than you
love yourself.
—*Josh Billings*

Dogs come when they're called; cats take a message and get
back to you.
—*Mary Bly*

If dogs talked, one of them would be president by now.
Everybody likes dogs.
— *Dean Koontz*

You call to a dog and a dog will break its neck to get to you.
Dogs just want to please. Call to a cat and its attitude is,
"What's in it for me?"
— *Lewis Grizzard*

Cat's motto: No matter what you've done wrong, always try
to make it look like the dog did it.
— *Anonymous*

I wonder if other dogs think poodles are members of a weird
religious cult.
— *Rita Rudner*

I have studied the wisdom of many philosophers and many
cats. The wisdom of cats is infinitely superior.
— *Hippolyte Taine*

A dog is a man's best friend. A cat is a cat's best friend.
— *Robert J. Vogel*

Animals

Dogs believe they are human. Cats believe they are God.
　　—Anonymous

Women and cats do as they please, and men and dogs might as well relax [and get used] to it.
　　—Robert A. Heinlein, in Glory Road

There's no psychiatrist in the world like a puppy licking your face.
　　—Bernard Williams

People that don't like cats haven't met the right one yet.
　　—Deborah A. Edwards

My husband said it was him or the cat...I miss him sometimes.
　　—Anonymous

When a man's best friend is his dog, that dog has a problem.
　　—Edward Abbey

[A cat] pours his body out on the floor like water.
　　—William Lyon Phelps

To err is human, to forgive, canine.
> —*Anonymous*

The better I get to know men, the more I find myself loving dogs.
> —*Charles de Gaulle, attributed*

I loathe people who keep dogs. They are cowards who haven't got the guts to bite people themselves.
> —*August Strindberg*

Life is a series of dogs.
> —*George Carlin*

When dogs leap on to your bed, it's because they adore being with you. When cats leap on to your bed, it's because they adore your bed.
> —*Alisha Everett*

Yesterday I was a dog. Today I'm a dog. Tomorrow I'll probably still be a dog. Sigh! There's so little hope for advancement.
> —*Snoopy, in* Peanuts *by Charles M. Schulz*

If you pick up a starving dog and make him prosperous, he will not bite you. This is the principal difference between a dog and a man.
> —*Mark Twain*

He that lieth down with dogs, shall rise up with fleas.
> —*Benjamin Franklin*

Nothing is so good for the inside of a man as the outside of a horse.
> —*Ronald Reagan [among others]*

Take most people, they're crazy about cars...I don't even like old cars. I mean they don't even interest me. I'd rather have a goddam horse. A horse is at least human, for God's sake.
> —*J. D. Salinger,* The Catcher in the Rye

Art

All art is quite useless.
> —*Oscar Wilde,* The Picture of Dorian Gray

I don't own any of my own paintings because a Picasso original costs several thousand dollars—it's a luxury I can't afford.
> —*Pablo Picasso*

I've finished that chapel I was painting. The Pope is quite satisfied.
> —*Michelangelo, on completing the ceiling of the Sistine Chapel*

Life is short, and art long.
> —*Hippocrates*

Abstract art is a product of the untalented, sold by the unprincipled to the utterly bewildered.
> —*Al Capp*

Any fool can paint a picture, but it takes a wise man to be able to sell it.
> —*Samuel Butler*

Art is the most beautiful of lies.
> —*Claude Debussy*

Art

There is no more somber enemy of good art than the pram in the hall.
> —*Cyril Connolly*

Buy old masters. They fetch a better price than old mistresses.
> —*Lord Beaverbrook*

But the Devil whoops, as he whooped of old: "It's clever, but is it art?"
> —*Rudyard Kipling*

Every time I paint a portrait I lose a friend.
> —*John Singer Sargent*

If Botticelli were alive today he'd be working for *Vogue*.
> —*Peter Ustinov*

There are moments when Art almost attains to the dignity of manual labor.
> —*Oscar Wilde,* The Model Millionaire

I think that 95 percent of what passes for art in this world is complete and utter shit. And 4 of the other 5 percent is shit with an asterisk. But oh, that 1 percent makes you proud to be a human, doesn't it?
—*Dennis Miller*

What garlic is to salad, insanity is to art.
—*Augustus Saint-Gaudens*

If that's art, I'm a Hottentot!
—*Harry S. Truman*

An artist is somebody who produces things that people don't need to have but that he—for *some reason*—thinks it would be a good idea to give them.
—*Andy Warhol*

You must have the devil in you to succeed in any of the arts.
—*Voltaire*

Art is making something out of nothing and selling it.
—*Frank Zappa*

Art

All bad art is the result of good intentions.
——*Oscar Wilde,* De Profundis

I would never have taken up painting if women did not have breasts.
——*Pierre-Auguste Renoir*

What is an artist? For every thousand people there's 900 doing the work, 90 doing well, nine doing good, and one lucky bastard who's the artist.
——*Tom Stoppard,* Travesties

The true artist will let his wife starve, his children go barefoot, his mother drudge for his living at 70, sooner than work at anything but his art.
——*George Bernard Shaw,* Man and Superman

One should either be a work of art, or wear a work of art.
——*Oscar Wilde*

It's amazing what you can do with an E in A-level art, a twisted imagination, and a chainsaw.
——*Damien Hirst, after winning the Turner Prize*

She is like most artists; she is all style without any sincerity.
—*Oscar Wilde,* The Nightingale and the Rose

Australia and Australians

To Australia? Oh, don't mention that dreadful vulgar place.
—*Oscar Wilde,* Lady Windermere's Fan

Racial characteristics: violently loud alcoholic roughnecks
whose idea of fun is to throw up on your car. The
national sport is breaking furniture and the average daily
consumption of beer in Sydney is ten and three-quarter
Imperial gallons for children under the age of nine.
—*P. J. O'Rourke*

New Zealanders who leave for Australia raise the IQ of
both countries.
—*Robert Muldoon*

I've been called a pommy bastard many times, but look
what it has done for me. If you want to develop character,
go to Australia.
—*Prince Charles*

I don't despair about the cultural scene in Australia because there isn't one here to despair about.
    —Robert Helpmann

Koala Triangle: a mysterious zone in the Southern Hemisphere where persons of talent disappear without trace.
    —Barry Humphries

When I look at the map and see what an ugly-looking country Australia is, I feel as if I want to go there to see if it cannot be changed into a more beautiful form.
    —Oscar Wilde, attributed

Where the hell is Australia anyway?
    —Britney Spears

If you find an Australian indoors, it's a fair bet that he will have a glass in his hand.
    —Jonathan Aitken

It's been like swimming in undiluted sewage.
    —Prince Charles, on St. Kilda Beach, in Melbourne

We may be a small race, but there's divinity in our cricket.
— *Thomas Keneally*

Melbourne is the kind of town that really makes you consider the question "Is there life after death?"
— *Bette Midler*

God made the harbor, and that's all right, but Satan made Sydney.
— *Citizen of Sydney, quoted by Mark Twain,* More Tramps Abroad

Beauty and Ugliness

Beauty, n. The power by which a woman charms a lover and terrifies a husband.
— *Ambrose Bierce,* The Devil's Dictionary

She is a peacock in everything but beauty.
— *Oscar Wilde,* The Picture of Dorian Gray

Beauty may be skin deep, but ugly goes clear to the bone.
— *Redd Foxx*

Beauty and Ugliness

Beauty is all very well at first sight; but who ever looks at it
when it has been in the house three days?
— *George Bernard Shaw,* Man and Superman

There are no ugly women, only lazy ones.
— *Helena Rubinstein*

She got her good looks from her father. He's a
plastic surgeon.
— *Groucho Marx*

Curious thing, plain women are always jealous of their
husbands, beautiful women never are!
— *Oscar Wilde,* A Woman of No Importance

I never see thy face but I think upon hell-fire.
— *William Shakespeare,* Henry IV, Part 1

A woman wants to be pretty rather than intelligent, because
men generally see better than they think.
— *Jewish proverb*

Where wilt thou find a cavern dark enough to mask thy monstrous visage?
—*William Shakespeare,* Julius Caesar

They [good looks] are a snare that every sensible man would like to be caught in.
—*Oscar Wilde,* The Importance of Being Earnest

Beauty is in the eye of the beer holder.
—*Anonymous*

Beauty is the first present nature gives to a woman and the first it takes away.
—*Fay Weldon*

...I think it is better to be beautiful than to be good. But...it is better to be good than to be ugly.
—*Oscar Wilde,* The Picture of Dorian Gray

Beauty is in the eye of the beholder, and it may be necessary from time to time to give a stupid or misinformed beholder a black eye!
—*Miss Piggy, in* The Muppet Show

Birth

They say men can never experience the pain of childbirth…
they can if you hit them in the goolies with a cricket bat for
fourteen hours.
— *Jo Brand*

I'm not interested in being Wonder Woman in the delivery
room. Give me drugs.
— *Madonna*

My first words as I was being born…I looked up at my
mother and said, "That's the last time I'm going up one of
those!"
— *Stephen Fry*

Somewhere on this globe, every ten seconds, there is
a woman giving birth to a child. She must be found
and stopped.
— *Sam Levenson*

Amnesia is a condition that enables a woman who has gone
through labor to have sex again.
— *Fran Lebowitz*

There is no cure for birth and death save to enjoy
the interval.
— *George Santayana*

The owl shriek'd at thy birth, an evil sign.
— *William Shakespeare,* Henry VI, Part 3

Birthdays

The best way to remember your wife's birthday is to forget
it once.
— *E. Joseph Cossman*

Birthdays are good for you. Statistics show that the people
who have the most live the longest.
— *Larry Lorenzoni*

A diplomat is a man who always remembers a woman's
birthday but never remembers her age.
— *Robert Frost*

Birthdays are nature's way of telling us to eat more cake.
— *Anonymous*

There is still no cure for the common birthday.
>   —*John Glenn*

Body

Curve: The loveliest distance between two points.
>   —*Mae West*

I have flabby thighs, but fortunately my stomach
covers them.
>   —*Joan Rivers*

My breasts are so versatile now—I can wear them down, up,
or side by side.
>   —*Cybill Shepherd*

In junior high, a boy poured water down my shirt and yelled,
"Now maybe they'll grow."
>   —*Pamela Anderson*

I have the body of an eighteen-year-old. I keep it in
the fridge.
>   —*Spike Milligan*

Looking at cleavage is like looking at the sun. You don't stare at it. It's too risky. You get a sense of it, and then you look away.
　　—Jerry Seinfeld

My bottom is so big it's got its own gravitational field.
　　—Carol Vorderman

Let me have men about me that are fat;
Sleek-headed men, and such as sleep o' nights.
　　—William Shakespeare, Julius Caesar

The average man is more interested in a woman who is interested in him than he is in a woman with beautiful legs.
　　—Marlene Dietrich

All I can say is, if they show my butt in a movie, it better be a wide shot.
　　—Jennifer Lopez

There are two reasons why I'm in show business, and I'm standing on both of them.
　　—Betty Grable

Body

A woman is as young as her knees.
—*Mary Quant*

The most popular image of the female despite the exigencies of the clothing trade is all boobs and buttocks, a hallucinating sequence of parabolae and bulges.
—*Germaine Greer*

Christians can have big tits, too.
—*Jane Russell*

I have little feet because nothing grows in the shade.
—*Dolly Parton*

There are three reasons for breastfeeding: The milk is always at the right temperature; it comes in attractive containers; and the cat can't get it.
—*Irena Chalmers*

If God had intended for breasts to be seen, He wouldn't have created large woolen pullovers.
—*Tracey Ullman*

My breasts have a career of their own. Theirs is going better.
   —*Jennifer Love Hewitt*

Working with Sophia Loren was like being bombed with watermelons.
   —*Alan Ladd*

The soul is born old but grows young. That is the comedy of life. And the body is born young and grows old. That is life's tragedy.
   —*Oscar Wilde,* A Woman of No Importance

If I see something sagging, bagging, and dragging, I'm going to nip it, tuck it, and suck it.
   —*Dolly Parton*

Your bum is the greatest thing about you.
   —*William Shakespeare,* Measure For Measure

Books and Reading

A classic is something that everybody wants to have read and nobody wants to read.
— *Mark Twain*

I took a speed-reading course and read *War and Peace* in 20 minutes. It involves Russia.
— *Woody Allen*

It is a good thing for an uneducated man to read books of quotations.
— *Winston Churchill*

There is no such thing as a moral or immoral book. Books are well written, or badly written. That is all.
— *Oscar Wilde,* The Picture of Dorian Gray

What really knocks me out is a book that, when you're all done reading it, you wish the author that wrote it was a terrific friend of yours and you could call him up on the phone whenever you felt like it.
— *J. D. Salinger,* The Catcher in the Rye

I honestly believe there is absolutely nothing wrong about going to bed with a good book…or a friend who's read one.
  —*Phyllis Diller*

Be careful about reading health books. You may die of a misprint.
  —*Mark Twain*

The good ended happily, and the bad unhappily. That is what Fiction means.
  —*Oscar Wilde,* The Importance of Being Earnest

Hiring someone to write your autobiography is like hiring someone to take a bath for you.
  —*Mae West*

Tell your nice mummies and daddies to buy this book for you and hit them until they do.
  —*Spike Milligan*

There are two motives for reading a book: one, that you enjoy it, the other that you can boast about it.
  —*Bertrand Russell*

I never travel without my diary. One should always have something sensational to read in the train.
  — *Oscar Wilde,* The Importance of Being Earnest

Times are bad. Children no longer obey their parents, and everyone is writing a book.
  — *Cicero*

Always read something that will make you look good if you die in the middle of it.
  — *P. J. O'Rourke*

Parents should leave books lying around marked "forbidden" if they want their children to read.
  — *Doris Lessing*

Every great man nowadays has his disciples, and it is always Judas who writes the biography.
  — *Oscar Wilde,* The Critic as Artist

Bushisms—
George W. Bush's Finest

They misunderestimated me.

Rarely is the question asked, is our children learning?

I have opinions of my own, strong opinions, but I don't always agree with them.

I know the human being and fish can coexist peacefully.

I know how hard it is for you to put food on your family.

Will the highways on the Internet become more few?

I don't do nuance.

I know what I believe. I will continue to articulate what I believe and what I believe—I believe what I believe is right.

I think anybody who doesn't think I'm smart enough to handle the job is underestimating.

I think war is a dangerous place.

I understand small business growth. I was one.

The problem with the French is that they don't have a word for entrepreneur.

I wish I wasn't the war president. Who in the heck wants to be a war president? I don't.

We ought to make the pie higher.

I think we agree, the past is over.

When I was a kid, I remember that they used to put out there in the Old West a "wanted" sign. It said, Wanted: Dead or Alive.

One of the great things about books is sometimes there are some fantastic pictures.

I promise to listen to what was said here, even though I wasn't here.

It will take time to restore chaos and order [in Iraq]—order out of chaos. But we will.

I hear there's rumors on the, uh, Internets….

If the terriers and bariffs are torn down, this economy will grow.

If this were a dictatorship, it would be a heck of a lot easier, just so long as I'm the dictator.

He can't take the high horse and then claim the low road.

I've coined new words, like "misunderstanding" and "Hispanically."

I'm also not very analytical. You know I don't spend a lot of time thinking about myself, about why I do things.

I think we ought to raise the age at which juveniles can have a gun.

I'm the master of low expectations.

More and more of our imports come from overseas.

Do you have blacks, too?
— *to then Brazilian President Fernando Cardoso*

It's clearly a budget. It's got a lot of numbers in it.

Too many OB/GYNs aren't able to practice their love with women all across this country.

Our enemies are innovative and resourceful, and so are we. They never stop thinking about new ways to harm our country and our people. And neither do we.

Families is where our nation finds hope, where wings take dream.

There's an old saying in Tennessee—I know it's in Texas, probably in Tennessee—that says, fool me once, shame on— shame on you. Fool me—you can't get fooled again.

First, let me make it very clear, poor people aren't necessarily killers. Just because you happen to be not rich doesn't mean you're willing to kill.

Home is important. It's important to have a home.

I am a person who recognizes the fallacy of humans.

The challenge facing the United States is that we have to be right one time. I mean 100% of the time.

And there's no doubt in my mind, not one doubt in my mind, that we will fail.

I think if you know what you believe, it makes it a lot easier to answer questions. I can't answer your question.

I want to thank my friend, Senator Bill Frist, for joining us today....He married a Texas girl, I want you to know. Karyn is with us. A West Texas girl, just like me.

The war on terror involves Saddam Hussein because of the nature of Saddam Hussein, the history of Saddam Hussein, and his willingness to terrorize himself.

As governor of Texas, I have set high standards for our public schools, and I have met those standards.

I don't think we need to be subliminable about the differences between our views on prescription drugs.

You teach a child to read, and he or her will be able to pass a literacy test.

It would be a mistake for the United States Senate to allow any kind of human cloning to come out of that chamber.

I'm honored to shake the hand of a brave Iraqi citizen who had his hand cut off by Saddam Hussein.

We cannot let terrorists and rogue nations hold this nation hostile or hold our allies hostile.

Africa is a nation that suffers from incredible disease.

This is still a dangerous world. It's a world of madmen and uncertainty and potential mental losses.

Keep good relations with the Grecians.

When I was young and irresponsible, I was young and irresponsible.

California

You haven't lived until you've died in California.
—*Mort Sahl*

California is a fine place to live—if you happen to be an orange.
—*Fred Allen*

I love California, I practically grew up in Phoenix.
—*Dan Quayle*

In California, they don't throw their garbage away—they make it into TV shows.
—*Woody Allen*

I love Los Angeles. I love Hollywood. They're beautiful. Everybody's plastic, but I love plastic. I want to be plastic.
—*Andy Warhol*

In California everyone goes to a therapist, is a therapist, or is a therapist going to a therapist.
—*Truman Capote*

In Los Angeles everyone has perfect teeth. It's
crocodile land.
      —*Gwyneth Paltrow*

The formula for a happy marriage? It's the same as the
one for living in California: when you find a fault, don't
dwell on it.
      —*Jay Trachman*

Fall is my favorite season in Los Angeles, watching the birds
change color and fall from the trees.
      —*David Letterman*

Adultery—which is the only grounds for divorce in New
York—is not grounds for divorce in California. As a matter of
fact, adultery in Southern California is grounds for marriage.
      —*Allan Sherman*

This is California. Blondes are like the state flower
or something.
      —*Ian Ziering as Steve Sanders, on*
        Beverly Hills 90210

[Beverly Hills is so exclusive]…even the police have an unlisted telephone number.
    —*Morey Amsterdam*

If a tidal wave hits LA, just grab a fake boob for safety.
    —*Sarah Michelle Gellar*

One of the things I had a hard time getting used to when I came to California in '78 was Santa Claus in shorts.
    —*Dennis Franz*

It is an odd thing, but every one who disappears is said to be seen at San Francisco. It must be a delightful city, and possess all the attractions of the next world.
    —*Oscar Wilde,* The Picture of Dorian Gray

One day if I do go to heaven, I'll look around and say, "It ain't bad, but it ain't San Francisco."
    —*Herb Caen*

Canada and Canadians

Canada is an entire country named Doug.
  — *Greg Proops*

Canada is a country so square that even the female impersonators are women.
  — *Richard Benner*

You have to know a man awfully well in Canada to know his surname.
  — *John Buchan*

A Canadian is sort of like an American, but without the gun.
  — *Anonymous*

Wherever you go in the world, you just have to say you're a Canadian and people laugh.
  — *John Candy*

The Canadian Prime Minister said Canada would lend the U.S. its full military support. You know what that means: both tanks.
　　—*Jay Leno*

America's attic, an empty room, a something possible, a chance, a dance that is not danced. A cold kingdom.
　　—*Patrick Anderson, "Poem on Canada" in*
　　The White Centre

Canada has never been a melting pot; more like a tossed salad.
　　—*Arnold Edinborough*

Canada is a country whose main exports are hockey players and cold fronts. Our main imports are baseball players and acid rain.
　　—*Pierre Trudeau*

Canada is the only country in the world that knows how to live without an identity.
　　—*Marshall McLuhan*

Canadians are Americans with no Disneyland.
　　—*Margaret Mahy*

Canada's national bird is the grouse.
— *Stuart Keate*

God Bless America, but God help Canada to put up
with them!
— *Anonymous*

Canada is useful only to provide me with furs.
— *Madame de Pompadour*

Canada is all right really, though not for the whole weekend.
— *Saki (H. H. Munro)*

...a few acres of snow...
— *Voltaire*

I don't even know what street Canada is on.
— *Al Capone*

In any world menu, Canada must be considered the
vichyssoise of nations—it's cold, half-French, and difficult
to stir.
— *Stuart Keate*

It's going to be a great country when they finish
unpacking it.
—*Andrew H. Malcom*

The beaver is a good national symbol for Canada. He's so
busy chewing he can't see what's going on.
—*Howard Cable*

Very little is known of the Canadian country since it
is rarely visited by anyone but the Queen and illiterate
sport fishermen.
—*P. J. O'Rourke*

The beaver, which has come to represent Canada as the
eagle does the United States and the lion Britain, is a
flat-tailed, slow-witted, toothy rodent known to bite off its
own testicles or to stand under its own falling trees.
—*June Callwood*

For some reason a glaze passes over people's faces when you
say "Canada."
—*Sondra Gotlieb*

Canada could have enjoyed: English government,
French culture, and American know-how. Instead it ended

up with English know-how, French government, and American culture.
— *John Colombo*

I get to go to lots of overseas places, like Canada.
— *Britney Spears, when asked what she enjoyed about touring*

It's not the end of the world, but you can see it from there.
— *Pierre Trudeau, on Edmonton, Alberta*

Children and Parenting

My mother loved children—she would have given anything if I had been one.
— *Groucho Marx*

To lose one parent may be regarded as a misfortune; to lose both looks like carelessness.
— *Oscar Wilde,* The Importance of Being Earnest

Children nowadays are tyrants. They contradict their parents, gobble their food, and tyrannize their teachers.
— *Socrates*

Children are a great comfort in your old age, and they help you reach it faster, too.
— *Lionel Kauffman*

Children really brighten up a household. They never turn the lights off.
— *Ralph Bus*

It kills you to see them grow up. But I guess it would kill you quicker if they didn't.
— *Barbara Kingsolver, in* Animal Dreams

The one thing children wear out faster than shoes is parents.
— *John J. Plomp*

If nature had arranged that husbands and wives should have children alternatively, there would never be more than three in a family.
— *Laurence Housman*

Adorable children are considered to be the general property of the human race. (Rude children belong strictly to their mothers.)
—*Miss Manners (Judith Martin)*

I figure when my husband comes home from work, if the kids are still alive, then I've done my job.
—*Roseanne Barr*

Sometimes, when I look at my children, I say to myself, "Lillian, you should have stayed a virgin."
—*Lillian Carter*

If your kids are giving you a headache, follow the directions on the aspirin bottle, especially the part that says "keep away from children."
—*Susan Savannah*

Like all parents, my husband and I just do the best we can, and hold our breath, and hope we've set aside enough money to pay for our kids' therapy.
—*Michelle Pfeiffer*

Raising kids is part joy and part guerrilla warfare.
—*Ed Asner*

You see much more of your children once they leave home.
— *Lucille Ball*

What is a home without children? Quiet.
— *Henny Youngman*

The trouble with children is that they are not returnable.
— *Quentin Crisp,* The Naked Civil Servant

A small boy is a noise with dirt on it.
— *Anonymous*

The baby is fine. The only problem is that he looks like
Edward G. Robinson.
— *Woody Allen*

If there were no schools to take the children from
home part of the time, the insane asylums would be filled
with mothers.
— *Edgar W. Howe*

There was never a child so lovely but his mother was glad to get him to sleep.
　　—Ralph Waldo Emerson

Before I got married, I had six theories about bringing up children; now I have six children and no theories.
　　—John Wilmot, Earl of Rochester

I want my children to have all the things I couldn't afford. Then I want to move in with them.
　　—Phyllis Diller

It is amazing how quickly the kids learn to drive a car, yet are unable to understand the lawnmower, snowblower, or vacuum cleaner.
　　—Ben Bergor

There are three ways to get something done: do it yourself, employ someone, or forbid your children to do it.
　　—Mona Crane

Always be nice to your children because they are the ones who will choose your rest home.
　　—Phyllis Diller

Children and Parenting

A child is a curly, dimpled lunatic.
>—*Ralph Waldo Emerson*

There's no such thing as a tough child. If you parboil them first for seven hours, they always come out tender.
>—*W. C. Fields*

If children grew up according to early indications, we should have nothing but geniuses.
>—*Johann Wolfgang von Goethe*

The best way to keep children home is to make the home atmosphere pleasant—and let the air out of the tires.
>—*Dorothy Parker*

The first half of our lives is ruined by our parents, and the second half by our children.
>—*Clarence Darrow*

Human beings are the only creatures on earth that allow their children to come back home.
>—*Bill Cosby*

You can learn many things from children. How much patience you have, for instance.
— *Franklin P. Jones*

I never met a kid I liked.
— *W. C. Fields*

The moment you have children yourself, you forgive your parents everything.
— *Susan Hill*

The most effective form of birth control I know is spending the day with my kids.
— *Jill Bensley*

Kids. They're not easy. But there has to be some penalty for sex.
— *Bill Maher*

You know your children are growing up when they stop asking you where they came from and refuse to tell you where they're going.
— *P. J. O'Rourke*

There are only two things a child will share willingly—
communicable diseases and his mother's age.
— *Dr. Benjamin Spock*

Any kid'll run any errand for you if you ask at bedtime.
— *Red Skelton*

Familiarity breeds contempt—and children.
— *Mark Twain,* Notebook

One hour with a child is like a ten-mile run.
— *Joan Benoit Samuelson*

My husband and I are either going to buy a dog or have
a child. We can't decide whether to ruin our carpet or ruin
our lives.
— *Rita Rudner*

Do not breed. Nothing gives less pleasure than childbearing.
Pregnancies are damaging to health, spoil the figure, wither
the charms, and it's the cloud of uncertitude forever hanging
over those events that darkens a husband's mood.
— *Marquis De Sade,* Juliette

Children begin by loving their parents; as they grow older they judge them; sometimes they forgive them.
> —*Oscar Wilde,* The Picture of Dorian Gray

Few parents nowadays pay any regard to what their children say to them. The old-fashioned respect for the young is fast dying out.
> —*Oscar Wilde,* The Importance of Being Earnest

If you really want to hear about it, the first thing you'll probably want to know is where I was born, and what my lousy childhood was like, and how my parents were occupied and all before they had me, and all that David Copperfield kind of crap, but I don't feel like going into it, if you want to know the truth.
> —*J. D. Salinger,* The Catcher in the Rye

Chocolate

It's not that chocolates are a substitute for love. Love is a substitute for chocolate. Chocolate is, let's face it, far more reliable than a man.
> —*Miranda Ingram*

There's nothing better than a good friend, except a good friend with chocolate.
— *Linda Grayson*

There are four basic food groups: milk chocolate, dark chocolate, white chocolate, and chocolate truffles.
— *Anonymous*

Chocolate is a divine, celestial drink, the sweat of the stars, the vital seed, divine nectar, the drink of the gods, panacea and universal medicine.
— *Geronimo Piperni*

I never met a chocolate I didn't like.
— *Marina Sirtis as Deanna Troi, on*
Star Trek: The Next Generation

Christmas

Aren't we forgetting the true meaning of Christmas? You know, the birth of Santa.
— *Bart Simpson, on* The Simpsons

A Merry Christmas to all my friends except two.
  —*W. C. Fields*

Santa Claus has the right idea—visit people only once
a year.
  —*Victor Borge*

Christmas, n. A day set apart and consecrated to gluttony,
drunkenness, maudlin sentiment, gift-taking, public dullness
and domestic behavior.
  —*Ambrose Bierce,* The Devil's Dictionary

The whole point of Christmas is that it is a debauch—as it
was probably long before the birth of Christ was arbitrarily
fixed at that date.
  —*George Orwell*

There are three stages of man: He believes in Santa Claus;
he does not believe in Santa Claus; he is Santa Claus.
  —*Bob Phillips*

Every idiot who goes about with "Merry Christmas" on his
lips, should be boiled with his own pudding, and buried with
a stake of holly through his heart.
  —*Charles Dickens,* A Christmas Carol

Christmas

What I don't like about office Christmas parties is looking
for a job the next day.
    —*Phyllis Diller*

Christmas begins about the first of December with an office
party and ends when you finally realize what you spent,
around April fifteenth of the next year.
    —*P. J. O'Rourke*

I never believed in Santa Claus because I knew no white
man would be coming into my neighborhood after dark.
    —*Dick Gregory*

The Supreme Court ruled against a nativity scene in
Washington, D.C. This wasn't for religious reasons. They
couldn't find three wise men and a virgin.
    —*Jay Leno*

Let me see if I've got this Santa business straight. You say he
wears a beard, has no discernible source of income, and flies
to cities all over the world under cover of darkness? You sure
this guy isn't laundering illegal drug money?
    —*Tom Armstrong*

Conversation

I love talking about nothing....It is the only thing I know anything about.
    —*Oscar Wilde,* An Ideal Husband

I often quote myself; it adds spice to my conversation.
    —*George Bernard Shaw*

I am so clever that sometimes I don't understand a single word of what I am saying.
    —*Oscar Wilde,* The Remarkable Rocket

I speak two languages, English and Body.
    —*Mae West*

She speaks, yet she says nothing.
    —*William Shakespeare,* Romeo and Juliet

"No comment" is a splendid expression. I'm using it again and again.
    —*Winston Churchill*

He speaks nothing but madman.
  —*William Shakespeare,* Twelfth Night

I think that whenever one has anything unpleasant to say,
one should always be quite candid.
  —*Oscar Wilde,* The Importance of Being Earnest

It is a much cleverer thing to talk nonsense than to listen
to it...
  —*Oscar Wilde,* The Importance of Being Earnest

Silence is the most perfect expression of scorn.
  —*George Bernard Shaw,* Back to Methuselah

Better to be silent and be thought a fool than to speak and
remove all doubt.
  —*Abraham Lincoln*

Death

One can survive everything nowadays, except death...
  —*Oscar Wilde,* A Woman of No Importance

It's not that I'm afraid to die. I just don't want to be there when it happens.
— *Woody Allen*

I am ready to meet my Maker. Whether my Maker is prepared for the ordeal of meeting me is another matter.
— *Winston Churchill*

I want to die before my wife, and the reason is this: If it is true that when you die, your soul goes up to judgment, I don't want my wife up there ahead of me to tell them things.
— *Bill Cosby*

Everybody wants to go to heaven, but nobody wants to die.
— *Joe Louis*

Either this man is dead or my watch is stopped.
— *Groucho Marx*

I don't want to achieve immortality through my work; I want to achieve immortality by not dying.
— *Woody Allen*

Don't let Krusty's death get you down, boy. People die all the time, just like that. Why, you could wake up dead tomorrow! Well, goodnight.
— *Homer Simpson, on* The Simpsons

For myself, I have never killed anybody, but I have many times read obituary notices with great satisfaction.
— *Clarence Darrow*

Although always prepared for martyrdom, I preferred that it be postponed.
— *Winston Churchill*

Boy, when you're dead, they really fix you up. I hope to hell when I *do* die somebody has sense enough to just dump me in the river or something. Anything except sticking me in a goddam cemetery. People coming and putting a bunch of flowers on your stomach on Sunday, and all that crap. Who wants flowers when you're dead? Nobody.
— *J. D. Salinger,* The Catcher in the Rye

Death would be a beautiful place if it looks like Brad Pitt.
— *Carmen Electra*

I refused to attend his funeral. But I wrote a very nice letter explaining that I approved of it.
— *Mark Twain, on hearing of the death of a corrupt politician*

There are worse things in life than death. Have you ever spent an evening with an insurance salesman?
— *Woody Allen*

Why is it that we rejoice at birth and grieve at a funeral? It is because we are not the person involved.
— *Mark Twain,* Pudd'nhead Wilson

Life is pleasant. Death is peaceful. It's the transition that's troublesome.
— *Isaac Asimov*

A single death is a tragedy, a million deaths is a statistic.
— *Joseph Stalin, attributed*

Death is not the end. There remains the litigation over the estate.
— *Ambrose Bierce*

...when a man knows he is to be hanged in a fortnight, it concentrates his mind wonderfully.
— *Samuel Johnson*

On the plus side, death is one of the few things that can be done as easily lying down.
— *Woody Allen*

Death will be a great relief. No more interviews.
— *Katharine Hepburn*

In this world nothing is certain but death and taxes.
— *Benjamin Franklin*

Ah...he'd make a lovely corpse!
— *Charles Dickens,* Martin Chuzzlewit

The only way you can become a legend is in your coffin.
— *Bette Davis*

If I had any decency, I'd be dead. Most of my friends are.
— *Dorothy Parker*

Education

To those of you who received honors, awards, and distinctions, I say, well done. And to the C students I say, you, too, can be president of the United States.
  —*George W. Bush*

He who can, does. He who cannot, teaches.
  —*George Bernard Shaw,* Man and Superman

Training is everything....Cauliflower is nothing but cabbage with a college education.
  —*Mark Twain,* Pudd'nhead Wilson

The more expensive a school is, the more crooks it has—I'm not kidding.
  —*J. D. Salinger,* The Catcher in the Rye

Society produces rogues and education makes one rogue cleverer than another.
  —*Oscar Wilde*

Education

I was thrown out of college for cheating on my metaphysics final….I looked within the soul of the boy sitting next to me.
   — *Woody Allen*

I have never let my schooling interfere with my education.
   — *Mark Twain*

I had a terrible education. I attended a school for emotionally disturbed teachers.
   — *Woody Allen*

Education is an admirable thing, but it is well to remember from time to time that nothing that is worth knowing can be taught.
   — *Oscar Wilde,* The Critic as Artist

Education: the path from cocky ignorance to miserable uncertainty.
   — *Mark Twain*

If all the girls attending [the Yale prom] were laid end to end, I wouldn't be at all surprised.
   — *Dorothy Parker*

Academe, n. An ancient school where morality and philosophy were taught. Academy, n. A modern school where football is taught.
— *Ambrose Bierce, The Devil's Dictionary*

England, Britain, and the English

The English contribution to world cuisine. The chip.
— *John Cleese,* A Fish Called Wanda

Sheep with a nasty side.
— *Cyril Connolly, on the British*

This Englishwoman is so refined
She has no bosom and no behind.
— *Stevie Smith*

In England there are 60 different religions, and only one sauce.
— *Francesco Caracciolo, attributed*

England, the heart of a rabbit in the body of a lion.
    —Eustache Deschamps

Carla: You're from England, huh?
Eric: How'd you guess?
Carla: Because you sound smart even when you say
stupid things.
    —Cheers

I sometimes think the only pleasure an Englishman has is in
passing on his cold germs.
    —Gerald Durrell, My Family and Other Animals

Continental people have sex lives; the English have hot-
water bottles.
    —George Mikes

I didn't know he was dead; I thought he was British.
    —Anonymous

Rain is the one thing the British do better than anybody else.
    —Marilyn French

…he is a typical Englishman, always dull and
usually violent.
> —*Oscar Wilde,* An Ideal Husband

The English instinctively admire any man who has no talent
and is modest about it.
> —*James Agate*

All Englishmen talk as if they've got a bushel of plums
stuck in their throats, and then, after swallowing them, get
constipated from the pits.
> —*W. C. Fields*

Englishmen never will be slaves: they are free to do whatever
the government and public opinion allow them to do.
> —*George Bernard Shaw,* Man and Superman

Britain is the society where the ruling class does not rule,
the working class does not work, and the middle class is not
in the middle.
> —*George Mikes,* English Humour for Beginners

The English have an extraordinary ability for flying into a
great calm.
> —*Alexander Woollcott*

…the British public are really not equal to the mental strain of having more than one topic every three months.
> — *Oscar Wilde,* The Picture of Dorian Gray

An Englishman thinks he is moral when he is only uncomfortable.
> — *George Bernard Shaw,* Man and Superman

I like the English. They have the most rigid code of immorality in the world.
> — *Malcolm Bradbury*

[My] roles play into a certain fantasy of what people want English people to be. Whereas half the time…we're vomiting beer and beating people up. I know I am.
> — *Hugh Grant*

There'll always be an England, even if it's in Hollywood.
> — *Bob Hope*

No Englishman is ever fairly beaten.
> — *George Bernard Shaw,* St. Joan

What a pity it is that we have no amusements in England but vice and religion!
— *Sydney Smith*

The Englishman has all the qualities of a poker except its occasional warmth.
— *Daniel O'Connell*

The English are not happy unless they are miserable...
— *George Orwell*

From every Englishman emanates a kind of gas, the deadly choke-lamp of boredom.
— *Heinrich Heine*

The most dangerous thing in the world is to make a friend of an Englishman, because he'll come sleep in your closet rather than spend ten shillings on a hotel.
— *Truman Capote*

[An Englishman] does everything on principle: He fights you on patriotic principles; he robs you on business principles; he enslaves you on imperial principles...
— *George Bernard Shaw,* The Man of Destiny

Silence can be defined as conversation with an Englishman.
　　—*Heinrich Heine*

The British have an umbilical cord which has never been cut and through which tea flows constantly. It is curious to watch them in times of sudden horror, tragedy, or disaster. The pulse stops apparently, and nothing can be done, and no move made, until "a nice cup of tea" is quickly made.
　　—*Marlene Dietrich*

There's nothing like an English weirdo. We have the best nutters in the world.
　　—*Sharon Osbourne*

If an Englishman gets run down by a truck, he apologizes to the truck.
　　—*Jackie Mason*

I know why the sun never sets on the British Empire. God wouldn't trust an Englishman in the dark.
　　—*J. Duncan Spaeth*

The British are so incestuous. They pass around partners as if they were passing popcorn at a movie.
　　—*Cameron Diaz*

Thinking is the most unhealthy thing in the world, and people die of it just as they die of any other disease. Fortunately, in England at any rate, thought is not catching.
　　—Oscar Wilde, The Decay of Lying

The English never smash in a face. They merely refrain from asking it to dinner.
　　—Margaret Halsey, With Malice Toward Some

Cricket—a game which the English, not being a spiritual people, have invented in order to give themselves some conception of eternity.
　　—Lord Mancroft

I think for my part one half of the nation is mad—and the other not very sound…
　　—Tobias Smollett, The Adventures of
　　　Sir Launcelot Greaves

What two ideas are more inseparable than Beer and Britannia?
　　—Sydney Smith

Mad dogs and Englishmen
Go out in the midday sun.
　　　—*Noël Coward*

If it is good to have one foot in England, it is still better, or at least as good, to have the other out of it.
　　　—*Henry James*

For 'tis a low, newspaper, humdrum, lawsuit Country…
　　　—*Lord Byron,* Don Juan

The English may not like music, but they absolutely love the noise it makes.
　　　—*Thomas Beecham*

We do not regard Englishmen as foreigners. We look on them only as rather mad Norwegians.
　　　—*Halvard Lange*

The English are not an inventive people; they don't eat enough pie.
　　　—*Thomas A. Edison*

The English have a miraculous power to change wine into water.
— *Oscar Wilde*

It is commonly observed that when two Englishmen meet, their first talk is of the weather.
— *Samuel Johnson*

You never find an Englishman among the underdogs—except in England, of course.
— *Evelyn Waugh*

You should study the Peerage, Gerald....It is the best thing in fiction the English have ever done.
— *Oscar Wilde,* A Woman of No Importance

On the Continent, people have good food; in England, people have good table manners.
— *George Mikes*

The whole strength of England lies in the fact that the enormous majority of the English people are snobs.
— *George Bernard Shaw,* Getting Married

England is a nation of shopkeepers.
> —*Napoleon Bonaparte [among others]*

Those comfortably padded lunatic asylums which are known, euphemistically, as the stately homes of England.
> —*Virginia Woolf*

I rode over the mountains to Huddersfield. A wilder people I never saw in England. The men, women, and children filled the streets as we rode along, and appeared just ready to devour us.
> —*John Wesley*

They are like their own beer; froth on top, dregs at the bottom, the middle excellent.
> —*Voltaire, on the British*

The English have three vegetables and two of them are cabbage.
> —*Walter Page*

Nearly every woman in England is competent to write an authoritative article on how not to cook cabbage.
> —*Vyvyan Holland*

The English never draw a line without blurring it.
  —*Winston Churchill*

We are a nation of governesses.
  —*George Bernard Shaw*

England is the paradise of women, the purgatory of men, and the hell of horses.
  —*John Florio*

I am happy now that Charles calls on my bedchamber less frequently than of old. As it is, I now endure but two calls a week, and when I hear his steps outside my door I lie down on my bed, close my eyes, open my legs and think of England.
  —*Lady Alice Hillingdon*

Family and Relations

I can't help detesting my relations. I suppose it comes from the fact that none of us can stand other people having the same faults as ourselves.
  —*Oscar Wilde*, The Picture of Dorian Gray

Families are like fudge—mostly sweet with a few nuts.
   —*Anonymous*

A family is a unit composed not only of children, but of
men, women, an occasional animal, and the common cold.
   —*Ogden Nash*

When our relatives are at home, we have to think of all their
good points or it would be impossible to endure them.
   —*George Bernard Shaw,* Heartbreak House

To the family—that dear octopus from whose tentacles
we never quite escape nor, in our inmost hearts, ever quite
wish to.
   —*Dodie Smith,* Dear Octopus

The Family! Home of all social evils, a charitable institution
for indolent women, a prison workshop for the slaving
breadwinner, and a hell for children.
   —*August Strindberg,* The Son of a Servant

I don't have to look up my family tree, because I know that
I'm the sap.
   —*Fred Allen*

Happiness is having a large, loving, caring, close-knit family in another city.
— *George Burns*

Watching your daughter being collected by her date feels like handing over a million-dollar Stradivarius to a gorilla.
— *Jim Bishop*

Have you ever had one of those days when you have had to murder a loved one because he is the devil?
— *Emo Philips*

I'm very proud of my gold pocket watch. My grandfather, on his deathbed, sold me this watch.
— *Woody Allen*

A lot of people would rather tour sewers than visit their cousins.
— *Jane Howard*

My grandmother started walking five miles a day when she was 60. She's 97 now, and we don't know where the hell she is.
— *Ellen DeGeneres*

I took my mother-in-law to Madame Tussaud's Chamber of Horrors and one of the attendants said "Keep her moving sir, we're stocktaking."
— *Les Dawson*

What ought to be done to the man who invented the celebrating of anniversaries? Mere killing would be too light.
— *Mark Twain*

Adam was the luckiest man in the world—he had no mother-in-law.
— *Sholom Aleichem*

The greater part of every family is always odious; if there are one or two good ones in a very large family, it is as much as can be expected.
— *Samuel Butler,* The Way of All Flesh

Behind every successful man stands a surprised mother-in-law.
— *Hubert Humphrey*

Remember. As far as anyone knows, we're a nice normal family.
— *Homer Simpson, on* The Simpsons

Be really good to your family and friends. You never know when you are going to need them to empty your bedpan.
—*Anonymous*

The reason grandchildren and grandparents get along so well is that they have a common enemy.
—*Sam Levenson*

I love hearing my relations abused. It is the only thing that makes me put up with them at all. Relations are simply a tedious pack of people, who haven't got the remotest knowledge of how to live, nor the smallest instinct about when to die.
—*Oscar Wilde*, The Importance of Being Earnest

Grandmas are moms with lots of frosting.
—*Anonymous*

Fashion and Clothes

A dress has no meaning unless it makes a men want to take it off.
—*Françoise Sagan*

I dress for women and I undress for men.
  —*Angie Dickinson*

Clothes make the man. Naked people have little or no influence on society.
  —*Mark Twain*

The only place men want depth in a woman is in her décolletage.
  —*Zsa Zsa Gabor*

All Americans dress well—they get their clothes in Paris.
  —*Oscar Wilde*

A woman's dress should be like a barbed-wire fence: serving its purpose without obstructing the view.
  —*Sophia Loren*

Women dress alike all over the world: They dress to be annoying to other women.
  —*Elsa Schiaparelli*

Friendship is not possible between two women, one of whom is very well dressed.
— *Laurie Colwin*

You can say what you like about long dresses, but they cover a multitude of shins.
— *Mae West*

Brevity is the soul of lingerie.
— *Dorothy Parker*

She was a curious woman, whose dresses always looked as if they had been designed in a rage and put on in a tempest.
— *Oscar Wilde,* The Picture of Dorian Gray

I wanted to be the first person to burn her bra, but it would have taken the fire department four days to put it out.
— *Dolly Parton*

Women's clothes: never wear anything that panics the cat.
— *P. J. O'Rourke*

Fashion is what one wears oneself. What is unfashionable is what other people wear.
— *Oscar Wilde,* An Ideal Husband

I would not be in some of your coats for twopence.
— *William Shakespeare,* Twelfth Night

Oh, the other night my wife met me at the front door wearing a see-through negligee. Unfortunately, she was just coming home.
— *Rodney Dangerfield*

Fashion is something that goes in one year and out the other.
— *Denise Klahn*

The Pope. Great guy. But in a fashion sense, he's one hat away from being Grand Wizard of the Ku Klux Klan.
— *Jon Stewart*

I have always felt a gift diamond shines so much better than one you buy for yourself.
— *Mae West*

From the artistic point of view, [fashion] is usually a
form of ugliness so intolerable that we have to alter it every
six months.
— *Oscar Wilde*

I base most of my fashion taste on what doesn't itch.
— *Gilda Radner*

Is there anything worn under the kilt? No, it's all in perfect
working order.
— *Spike Milligan*

I figure if high heels were so wonderful, men would be
wearing them.
— *Sue Grafton*

You ought to get out of those wet clothes and into a
dry martini.
— *Mae West, in* Every Day's a Holiday

One snap of my fingers, and I can raise hemlines so high,
the whole world's your gynecologist.
— *Joanna Lumley as Patsy Stone, on*
Absolutely Fabulous

With an evening coat and a white tie…anybody, even a stockbroker, can gain a reputation for being civilized.
— *Oscar Wilde,* The Picture of Dorian Gray

Big girls need big diamonds.
— *Elizabeth Taylor*

Food

In general, my children refuse to eat anything that hasn't danced on television.
— *Erma Bombeck*

Food is like sex: When you abstain, even the worst stuff begins to look good.
— *Beth McCollister*

I just love Chinese food. My favorite dish is number 27.
— *Clement Attlee*

I will not eat oysters. I want my food dead. Not sick. Not wounded. Dead.
— *Woody Allen*

Anyone who eats three meals a day should understand why cookbooks outsell sex books three to one.
> —*L. M. Boyd*

If God did not intend for us to eat animals, then why did he make them out of meat?
> —*John Cleese [among others]*

A woman should never be seen eating or drinking, unless it be lobster salad and champagne, the only true feminine and becoming viands.
> —*Lord Byron*

Behind every successful woman…is a substantial amount of coffee.
> —*Stephanie Piro*

Bread and butter, please. Cake is rarely seen at the best houses nowadays.
> —*Oscar Wilde,* The Importance of Being Earnest

I never worry about diets. The only carrots that interest me are the number you get in a diamond.
> —*Mae West*

Chopsticks are one of the reasons the Chinese never invented custard.
　　—*Spike Milligan*

Food is an important part of a balanced diet.
　　—*Fran Lebowitz*

I personally stay away from natural foods. At my age, I need all the preservatives I can get.
　　—*George Burns*

I never drink water, because fish fuck in it.
　　—*W. C. Fields*

I worry about scientists discovering someday that lettuce has been fattening all along.
　　—*Erma Bombeck*

Two cannibals eating a clown. One says to the other, "Does this taste funny to you?"
　　—*Tommy Cooper*

What would life be without coffee? But then, what is it even with coffee?
—*King Louis XV*

Men like to barbecue. Men will cook if danger is involved.
—*Rita Rudner*

Everything you see I owe to spaghetti.
—*Sophia Loren*

There is no love sincerer than the love of food.
—*George Bernard Shaw*

Beulah, peel me a grape.
—*Mae West, in* I'm No Angel

I asked the waiter, "Is this milk fresh?" He said, "Lady, three hours ago it was grass."
—*Phyllis Diller*

Once, during Prohibition, I was forced to live for days on nothing but food and water.
—*W. C. Fields*

What else is there to live for? Chinese food and women.
There is nothing else!
    —*Dudley Moore*

The most dangerous food is wedding cake.
    —*American saying*

Health food makes me sick.
    —*Calvin Trillin*

He was a bold man that first did eat an oyster.
    —*Jonathan Swift*

The odds of going to the store for a loaf of bread and coming
out with *only* a loaf of bread are three billion to one.
    —*Erma Bombeck*

Put all your eggs in one basket—and then watch that basket!
    —*Mark Twain,* Pudd'nhead Wilson

I never drink coffee at lunch—I find it keeps me awake for
the afternoon.
    —*Ronald Reagan*

Please, sir, I want some more.
  —*Charles Dickens,* Oliver Twist

Forgiveness

Men forget but never forgive. Women forgive but never forget.
  —*Anonymous*

Always forgive your enemies. Nothing annoys them so much.
  —*Oscar Wilde*

Beware of the man who does not return your blow: he neither forgives you nor allows you to forgive yourself.
  —*George Bernard Shaw,* Man and Superman

There is no revenge so complete as forgiveness.
  —*Josh Billings*

Forgive your enemies, but never forget their names.
  —*John F. Kennedy*

France and the French

If the French were really intelligent, they'd speak English.
—*Wilfrid Sheed*

The French are sawed-off sissies who eat snails and slugs and cheese that smells like people's feet. Utter cowards who force their own children to drink wine, they gibber like baboons even when you try to speak to them in their own wimpy language.
—*P. J. O'Rourke*

The French invented the only known cure for dandruff. It is called the guillotine.
—*P. G. Wodehouse*

The best thing I know between France and England is— the sea.
—*Douglas Jerrold*

No matter how politely or distinctly you ask a Parisian a question, he will persist in answering you in French.
—*Fran Lebowitz*

[I always eat at the Eiffel Tower restaurant] because it's the only place in Paris where I can avoid seeing the damned thing.
— *William Morris*

France has neither winter nor summer nor morals—apart from these drawbacks it is a fine country.
— *Mark Twain*

France: how can you govern a country that produces 265 varieties of cheese?
— *Charles de Gaulle*

I can never forgive God for creating the French.
— *Peter Ustinov*

France seems to interest herself mainly in high art and seduction.
— *Mark Twain*

France is a country where the money falls apart in your hands and you can't tear the toilet paper.
— *Billy Wilder*

To err is human. To loaf is Parisian.
  —*Victor Hugo*

In Paris they just simply opened their eyes and stared when we spoke to them in French! We never did succeed in making those idiots understand their own language.
  —*Mark Twain,* Innocents Abroad

France is a dog-hole.
  —*William Shakespeare,* All's Well That Ends Well

He can speak French; and therefore he is a traitor.
  —*William Shakespeare,* Henry VI, Part 2

Friends and Enemies

True friends stab you in the front.
  —*Oscar Wilde*

A friend in need is a friend to be avoided.
  —*Lord Samuel*

It's the friends you can call up at 4 a.m. that matter.
— *Marlene Dietrich*

The lion and the calf shall lie down together, but the calf won't get much sleep.
— *Woody Allen*

Your [real] friend is the man who knows all about you, and still likes you.
— *Elbert Hubbard*

One loyal friend is worth ten thousand relatives.
— *Euripides*

A true friend is one who overlooks your failures and tolerates your successes.
— *Doug Larson*

A real friend is one who walks in when the rest of the world walks out.
— *Walter Winchell*

A good friend is cheaper than therapy.
    —Anonymous

The Bible tells us to forgive our enemies; not our friends.
    —Margot Asquith

A true friend is someone who thinks that you are a good egg though he knows that you are slightly cracked.
    —Bernard Meltzer

My mother used to say there are no strangers, only friends you haven't met yet. She's now in a maximum-security twilight home in Australia.
    —Barry Humphries, as Dame Edna Everage

Whenever a friend succeeds, a little something in me dies.
    —Gore Vidal

The proper office of a friend is to side with you when you are in the wrong. Nearly anybody will side with you when you are in the right.
    —Mark Twain

A man cannot be too careful in the choice of his enemies.
— *Oscar Wilde*, The Picture of Dorian Gray

Love your enemy. But don't forget he is not your friend.
— *Paulo Coelho*

Keep your friends close, and your enemies closer.
— *Sun Tzu*

There are three faithful friends—an old wife, an old dog, and ready money.
— *Benjamin Franklin*

He's the kind of man who picks his friends—to pieces.
— *Mae West*

There is no spectacle more agreeable than to observe an old friend fall from a rooftop.
— *Confucius*

A friend is someone with whom you dare to be yourself.
— *Frank Crane*

Friends and Enemies

A friend can tell you things you don't want to tell yourself.
—*Frances Ward Weller,* Boat Song

A true friend never gets in your way unless you happen to be going down.
—*Arnold H. Glasow*

He has not an enemy in the world, and none of his friends like him.
—*Oscar Wilde, on George Bernard Shaw*

It takes your enemy and your friend, working together, to hurt you to the heart: the one to slander you and the other to get the news to you.
—*Mark Twain,* Following the Equator

After all, one can't complain. I have my friends. Somebody spoke to me only yesterday.
—*Eeyore, in* Winnie-the-Pooh *by A. A. Milne*

I choose my friends for their good looks, my acquaintances for their good characters, and my enemies for their good intellects.
—*Oscar Wilde,* The Picture of Dorian Gray

Gaffes and Dumbest Things Ever Said

What's Wal-Mart? Do they sell, like wall stuff?
  —*Paris Hilton*

I've never really wanted to go to Japan, simply because I don't really like eating fish, and I know that's very popular out there in Africa...
  —*Britney Spears*

The future will be better tomorrow.
  —*Dan Quayle*

Chuck, stand up, let the people see you.
  —*Joe Biden, to a man in a wheelchair*

If you stay here much longer, you'll all be slitty-eyed.
  —*Prince Philip, to a group of British students in China*

My fellow Americans, I'm pleased to tell you today that I've signed legislation that will outlaw Russia forever. We begin bombing in five minutes.

> —*Ronald Reagan, testing the microphone before a broadcast*

Every prime minister needs a Willie.

> —*Margaret Thatcher, referring to William Whitelaw*

I feel my best when I'm happy.

> —*Winona Ryder*

I'm not anorexic. I'm from Texas. Are there people from Texas who are anorexic? I've never heard of one. And that includes me.

> —*Jessica Simpson*

I think God is a giant vibrator in the sky...a pulsating force of incredible energy.

> —*David Arquette*

I have made good judgments in the past. I have made good judgments in the future.

> —*Dan Quayle*

A man I'm proud to call my friend. A man who will be the next president of the United States—Barack America!
> —*Joe Biden, at the first presidential campaign rally with Barack Obama*

I've now been in 57 states—I think one left to go.
> —*Barack Obama*

You managed not to get eaten, then?
> —*Prince Philip, to a British student who had been in Papua New Guinea*

I'm the Hiroshima of love.
> —*Sylvester Stallone*

Forget it, Louis. No Civil War picture ever made a nickel.
> —*MGM producer Irving Thalberg, to boss Louis B. Mayer, turning down a chance to make the film version of* Gone With the Wind

We don't like their sound. Groups of guitars are on the way out.
> —*Decca Recording Company executive, turning down the Beatles, 1962*

I tell you flatly, he can't last.
> —*Jackie Gleason, of Elvis Presley*

We're more popular than Jesus now; I don't know which will go first—rock and roll or Christianity.
> —*John Lennon*

We are not interested in science fiction which deals with negative utopias. They do not sell.
> —*Rejection letter to Stephen King for* Carrie

So, where's the Cannes Film Festival being held this year?
> —*Christina Aguilera*

I think gay marriage is something that should be between a man and a woman.
> —*Arnold Schwarzenegger*

All homosexuals should be castrated.
> —*Billy Graham, who later apologized for the remark*

I did not have sexual relations with that woman.
> —*Bill Clinton, denying he had sex with White House intern Monica Lewinsky*

You can't have been here that long—you haven't got a pot belly.
> —*Prince Philip, to a Briton in Budapest*

I suppose a knighthood is out of the question now?
> —*Spike Milligan, in a fax to Prince Charles after he called him a "little groveling bastard"*

Then you add two forkfuls of cooking oil.
> —*Julia Child*

I made a misstatement and I stand by all my misstatements.
> —*Dan Quayle*

I don't diet. I just don't eat as much as I'd like to.
> —*Linda Evangelista*

Movies are a fad. Audiences really want to see live actors on a stage.
> —*Charlie Chaplin*

It will be gone by June.
>—Variety *magazine, on rock and roll, 1955*

TV won't last because people will soon get tired of staring at a plywood box every night.
>—*Darryl Zanuck, 20th Century Fox movie studio head, 1946*

...there are no "knowns." There are things we know that we know. There are known unknowns. That is to say, there are things that we now know we don't know. But there are also unknown unknowns. There are things we don't know we don't know.
>—*Donald Rumsfeld*

Who the hell wants to hear actors talk? The music, that's the big plus.
>—*Harry Warner, Warner Brothers movie studio head, when asked about sound in films, 1927*

I'm just glad it'll be Clark Gable who's falling on his face, and not Gary Cooper.
>—*Gary Cooper, on his decision not to take the leading role in* Gone With The Wind

What a waste it is to lose one's mind, or not to have a mind is being very wasteful…
> — *Dan Quayle, mangling the United Negro College Fund's slogan, "A mind is a terrible thing to waste."*

I owe a lot to my parents, especially my mother and father.
> — *Greg Norman*

British women can't cook.
> — *Prince Philip*

Can't act, slightly bald, also dances.
> — *RKO Pictures screen test, comments about Fred Astaire*

You're next, loudmouth.
> — *Sonny Liston, to Cassius Clay*

Ghastly.
> — *Prince Philip, on Beijing, China, during an official trip there*

Sure there have been injuries and deaths in boxing—but none of them serious.
   —*Alan Minter*

Radio has no future.
   —*Lord Kelvin, British mathematician
   and physicist, 1897*

China is a big country, inhabited by many Chinese.
   —*Charles de Gaulle*

We don't come here for our holidays. We can think of other ways of enjoying ourselves.
   —*Prince Philip, on Canada*

I was asked to come to Chicago because Chicago is one of our 52 states.
   —*Raquel Welch*

It is wonderful to be here in the great state of Chicago.
   —*Dan Quayle, attributed*

Today, nothing.
> —*King Louis XVI of France, in diary entry for*
> *July 14, 1789, the day the Bastille was stormed*

This is the greatest week in the history of the world since the Creation.
> —*Richard Nixon, welcoming back the crew of*
> *Apollo 11 from the first moon landing, 1969*

Man will never reach the moon regardless of all future scientific advances.
> —*Lee De Forest, inventor, 1957*

Heavier-than-air flying machines are impossible.
> —*Lord Kelvin, British mathematician*
> *and physicist, 1895*

Rail travel at high speed is not possible because passengers, unable to breathe, would die of asphyxia.
> —*Dr. Dionysius Lardner, Irish scientific writer, 1845*

You are a woman, aren't you?
> —*Prince Philip, accepting a gift from a*
> *Kenyan woman*

Of all the things I've lost, it's my mind I miss the most.
—*Ozzy Osbourne*

Gaiety is the most outstanding feature of the Soviet Union.
—*Joseph Stalin*

I don't see much future for the Americans...Everything about the behavior of American society reveals that it's half Judaized, and the other half negrified. How can one expect a state like that to hold together—a country where everything is built on the dollar?
—*Adolf Hitler*

I experimented with marijuana a time or two and I didn't like it. I didn't inhale. I never tried it again.
—*Bill Clinton*

It's no exaggeration to say that the undecideds could go one way of the other.
—*George H. W. Bush*

A zebra does not change its spots.
—*Al Gore, attacking President Bush, 1992*

I was known as the chief graverobber of my state.
— *Dan Quayle*

When the Paris Exhibition closes, the electric light will close with it, and very little more will be heard about it.
— *Professor Erasmus Wilson, 1878*

There is no reason for any individual to have a computer in the home.
— *Ken Olsen, president of Digital Equipment Corporation, 1977*

If it has got four legs and it is not a chair, if it has got two wings and it flies but is not an airplane, and if it swims and it is not a submarine, the Cantonese will eat it.
— *Prince Philip*

Always be sincere, even if you don't mean it.
— *Harry S. Truman*

We have become a grandmother.
— *Margaret Thatcher, announcing birth of her grandson Michael*

We understand the importance of having the bondage between the parent and the child.
— *Dan Quayle*

I believe that people would be alive today if there were a death penalty.
— *Nancy Reagan*

Had Christ died in my van, with people around Him who loved Him...it would be far more dignified. In my rusty van.
— *Euthanasia activist Dr. Jack Kevorkian*

Antichrist! I renounce you and all your cults and creeds.
— *Ian Paisley shouting at Pope John Paul II in Strasbourg*

I don't go so far as to think that the only good Indians are dead Indians, but I believe nine out of every ten are, and I shouldn't inquire too closely into the case of the tenth.
— *Theodore Roosevelt*

Airplanes are interesting toys, but of no military value.
— *Ferdinand Foch, Commandant, École Supérieure de Guerre, 1911*

I have determined that there is no market for talking pictures.
      — Thomas A. Edison, 1926

While theoretically and technically television may be feasible, commercially and financially, I consider it an impossibility, a development of which we need waste little time dreaming.
      — Lee De Forest, inventor, 1926

Try another profession. Any other.
      — Head of John Murray Anderson Drama School,
        to a young Lucille Ball

Far too noisy, my dear Mozart. Far too many notes.
      — Emperor Ferdinand of Austria, after hearing
      The Marriage of Figaro

Fiction writing is great, you can make up almost anything.
      — Ivana Trump

My dear sir, I have read your manuscript. Oh, my dear sir.
      — Rejection letter to Oscar Wilde for
      Lady Windermere's Fan

Who is this [Alexander] Pope that I hear so much about? I cannot discover what is his merit. Why will not my subjects write in prose! I hear a great deal too about Shakespeare, but I cannot read him, he is such a bombast fellow.
> —*King George II, attributed*

Everything that can be invented has been invented.
> —*Charles H. Duell, Commissioner of U.S. Office of Patents, 1899*

Although it is…an interesting novelty, the telephone has no commercial application.
> —*J. P. Morgan, to Alexander Graham Bell*

The Holocaust was an obscene period in our nation's history. I mean in this century's history. But we all lived in this century. I didn't live in this century.
> —*Dan Quayle*

Aren't most of you descended from pirates?
> —*Prince Philip, to an inhabitant of Cayman Islands*

I would like to spank director Spike Jonze.
> —*Meryl Streep, misreading a faxed acceptance speech at BAFTA awards*

Space travel is utter bilge.
—*Richard Wooley, Astronomer Royal of*
Great Britain, 1956

You'd better learn secretarial work or else get married.
—*Emmeline Snively, modeling agent, to*
Marilyn Monroe, 1944

You ain't goin' nowhere, son. You ought to go back to drivin'
a truck.
—*Jim Denny, manager of* Grand Ole Opry,
to Elvis Presley, 1954

America will soon observe the twentieth anniversary of
Neil Armstrong and Buzz Lukens walking on the moon.
—*Dan Quayle, confusing convicted sex offender/*
congressman Buzz Lukens with moonwalker
Buzz Aldrin

When the president does it, that means that it is not illegal.
—*Richard Nixon, 1977*

A third-rate burglary attempt not worthy of further White House comment.
> —*Ron Ziegler, White House press spokesman, on the Watergate break-in*

The girl doesn't, it seems to me, have a special perception or feeling which would lift that book above the curiosity level.
> —*Rejection note for* The Diary of Anne Frank

Stocks have reached what looks like a permanently high plateau.
> —*Irving Fisher, Professor of Economics, Yale University, October 17, 1929*

I have had 10,000 women since the age of thirteen and a half...I have not the slightest sexual vice, but I have the need to communicate.
> —*Georges Simenon*

Are you Indian or Pakistani? I can never tell the difference between you chaps.
> —*Prince Philip, at a reception for Commonwealth members*

Well-informed people know it is impossible to transmit the voice over wires as may be done with dots and dashes and signals of the Morse code, and that were it possible to do so, the thing would be of no practical value.
> —*Editorial in the* Boston Post, *1865*

It's only a toy.
> —*Gardiner Greene Hubbard, future father-in-law of Alexander Graham Bell, on seeing Bell's telephone, 1876*

I don't believe in black majority rule ever in Rhodesia, not in a thousand years.
> —*Ian Smith*

This president is going to lead us out of this recovery. It will happen.
> —*Dan Quayle*

The monarchy system adds gaiety to politics.
> —*Prince Philip*

If Beethoven's Seventh Symphony is not by some means abridged, it will soon fall into disuse.
> —*Philip Hale, Boston music critic, 1837*

It is impossible to sell animal stories in the USA…the choice of pigs as the ruling caste will no doubt give offense to many people, and particularly to anyone who is a bit touchy, as undoubtedly the Russians are.
— *Rejection letter to George Orwell for* Animal Farm

For NASA, space is still a high priority.
— *Dan Quayle*

X-rays will prove to be a hoax.
— *Lord Kelvin, British mathematician and physicist, 1896*

My friends, no matter how rough the road may be, we can and we will, never, never surrender to what is right.
— *Dan Quayle*

I love sports. Whenever I can, I always watch the Detroit Tigers on the radio.
— *Gerald R. Ford*

I'm not going to have some reporters pawing through our papers. We are the president.
— *Hillary Clinton, on the release of subpoenaed documents*

One word sums up probably the responsibility of any vice-president, and that one word is "to be prepared."
— *Dan Quayle*

I don't read books, I write them.
— *Henry Kissinger*

A long, dull novel about an artist…
— *Rejection letter to Irving Stone for* Lust for Life

We're going to have the best-educated Americans people in the world.
— *Dan Quayle*

It does not seem to us that you have been wholly successful in working out an admittedly promising idea.
— *Rejection letter to William Golding for* Lord of the Flies

I don't think anyone should write his autobiography until after he is dead.
— *Samuel Goldwyn*

Illegitimacy is something we should talk about in terms of not having it.
—*Dan Quayle*

I did not have 3,000 pairs of shoes. I had 1,060.
—*Imelda Marcos*

Who would want to see a play about an unhappy traveling salesman?
—*Cheryl Crawford, Broadway producer,*
turning down Arthur Miller's Death of a Salesman

[It's] time for the human race to enter the solar system.
—*Dan Quayle*

What do you gargle with, pebbles?
—*Prince Philip, to singer Tom Jones*

The problem with television is that people must sit and keep their eyes glued to the screen; the average American family hasn't time for it. Therefore, the showmen are convinced that…television will never be a serious competitor of broadcasting.
—*1939 editorial in the* New York Times

Germany and Germans

Oh *German*! I'm sorry. I thought there was something wrong with you.
> —*John Cleese as Basil Fawlty, on* Fawlty Towers

Racial characteristics: Piggish-looking, sadomasochistic automatons whose only known forms of relaxation are swilling watery beer from vast tubs and singing the idiotically repetitive verses of their porcine folk tunes....Their language lacks any semblance of civilized speech. Their usual diet consists almost wholly of old cabbage and sections of animal intestines filled with blood and gore.
> —*P. J. O'Rourke, "Foreigners Around the World,"* National Lampoon

They're Germans. Don't mention the war.
> —*John Cleese as Basil Fawlty, on* Fawlty Towers

German is a most extravagantly ugly language. It sounds like someone using a sick bag on a 747.
> —*William Rushton*

The Germans are exceedingly fond of Rhine wines; they are put up in tall, slender bottles, and are considered a pleasant beverage. One tells them from vinegar by the label.
  — *Mark Twain,* A Tramp Abroad

Waiting for the German verb is surely the ultimate thrill!
  — *Flann O'Brien*

The German people are an orderly, vain, deeply sentimental and rather insensitive people. They seem to feel at their best when they are singing in chorus, saluting or obeying orders.
  — *H. G. Wells,* Travels of a Republican Radical in Search of Hot Water

My husband's German. Every night I get dressed up as Poland and he invades me.
  — *Bette Midler*

You can always reason with a German. You can always reason with a barnyard animal, too, for all the good it does.
  — *P. J. O'Rourke,* Holidays in Hell

Life is too short to learn German.
  — *Richard Porson [among others]*

Whenever the literary German dives into a sentence, that is the last you are going to see of him till he emerges on the other side of his Atlantic with his verb in his mouth.
— *Mark Twain,* A Connecticut Yankee in King Arthur's Court

Why didn't the armistice treaty require the Germans to lay down their accordions along with their arms?
— *Bill Bryson*

Now, whatever music sounds like, I am glad to say that it does not sound in the smallest degree like German.
— *Oscar Wilde,* The Critic as Artist

According to a new survey, Germans are the best-behaved tourists in the world....it's only when they march into your country and want to stay forever, that's when it gets testy.
— *Jay Leno*

Happiness

Some cause happiness wherever they go; others whenever they go.
— *Oscar Wilde*

But a lifetime of happiness! No man alive could bear it: it would be hell on earth.
— *George Bernard Shaw,* Man and Superman

It isn't necessary to be rich and famous to be happy. It's only necessary to be rich.
— *Alan Alda*

Happiness, n. An agreeable sensation arising from contemplating the misery of another.
— *Ambrose Bierce,* The Devil's Dictionary

My Zen teacher also said: the only way to true happiness is to live in the moment and not worry about the future. Of course, he died penniless and single.
— *Sarah Jessica Parker as Carrie Bradshaw, on* Sex and the City

The search for happiness is one of the chief sources of unhappiness.
— *Eric Hoffer*

Nothing ages like happiness.
— *Oscar Wilde,* An Ideal Husband

Health and Sickness

Money cannot buy health, but I'd settle for a diamond-studded wheelchair.
— *Dorothy Parker*

I enjoy convalescence. It is the part that makes the illness worth while.
— *George Bernard Shaw,* Back to Methuselah

The best cure for hypochondria is to forget about your body and get interested in somebody else's.
— *Goodman Ace*

Thinking is the most unhealthy thing in the world, and people die of it just as they die of any other disease.
— *Oscar Wilde,* The Decay of Lying

The most infectious pestilence upon thee!
— *William Shakespeare,* Antony and Cleopatra

Never go to a doctor whose office plants have died.
— *Erma Bombeck*

Quit worrying about your health. It'll go away.
  —*Robert Orben*

The ideal way to get rid of any infectious disease would be to shoot instantly every person who comes down with it.
  —*H. L. Mencken*

Warning: Humor may be hazardous to your illness.
  —*Ellie Katz*

The best doctors in the world are Doctor Diet, Doctor Quiet, and Doctor Merryman.
  —*Jonathan Swift*

"Virus" is a Latin word used by doctors to mean, "Your guess is as good as mine."
  —*Anonymous*

History

History will be kind to me for I intend to write it.
  —*Winston Churchill*

History is bunk.
— *Henry Ford*

Anybody can make history. Only a great man can write it.
— *Oscar Wilde,* The Critic as Artist

History is the sum total of all the things that could have been avoided.
— *Konrad Adenauer*

History never repeats itself. The historians repeat each other. There is a wide difference.
— *Oscar Wilde*

History is a set of lies agreed upon.
— *Napoleon Bonaparte*

The one duty we owe to history is to rewrite it.
— *Oscar Wilde,* The Critic as Artist

Home

All I need is room enough to lay a hat and a few friends.
    —Dorothy Parker

Home life as we understand it is no more natural to us than
a cage is natural to a cockatoo.
    —George Bernard Shaw, Getting Married

A girl phoned me the other day and said, "Come on over;
nobody's home." I went over. Nobody was home.
    —Rodney Dangerfield

Home is the place where, when you have to go there,
They have to take you in.
    —Robert Frost

Home is the girl's prison and the woman's workhouse.
    —George Bernard Shaw, Man and Superman

There's no place like home—after the other places close.
    —Joe Laurie, Jr.

Home is where you hang your head.
—*Groucho Marx*

The great advantage of a hotel is that it's a refuge from
home life...
—*George Bernard Shaw,* You Never Can Tell

Husbands and Wives

Basically my wife was immature. I'd be in my bath, and she'd
come in and sink my boats.
—*Woody Allen*

Never trust a husband too far, nor a bachelor too near.
—*Helen Rowland*

Take my wife—please!
—*Henny Youngman*

The Ideal Husband? There couldn't be such a thing.
The institution is wrong.
—*Oscar Wilde,* A Woman of No Importance

I have learned that only two things are necessary to keep one's wife happy. First, let her think she is having her own way. And second, let her have it.
  — *Lyndon B. Johnson*

You mean apart from my own?
  — *Zsa Zsa Gabor, asked how many husbands she had had*

My wife and I were happy for 20 years. Then we met.
  — *Rodney Dangerfield*

It's most dangerous nowadays for a husband to pay any attention to his wife in public. It always makes people think that he beats her when they're alone.
  — *Oscar Wilde,* Lady Windermere's Fan

I haven't spoken to my wife in years. I didn't want to interrupt her.
  — *Rodney Dangerfield*

A husband is what is left of a lover, after the nerve has been extracted.
  — *Helen Rowland,* A Guide to Men

When a man opens the car door for his wife, it's either a new car or a new wife.
— *Prince Philip*

My wife has a slight impediment in her speech. Every now and then she stops to breathe.
— *Jimmy Durante*

An archaeologist is the best husband any woman can have; the older she gets, the more interested he is in her.
— *Agatha Christie*

I'm a very committed wife. I should be committed, too, for being married so many times.
— *Elizabeth Taylor*

I wouldn't trust my husband with a young woman for five minutes, and he's been dead for 25 years.
— *Kathleen Behan*

The man who says his wife can't take a joke, forgets that she took him.
— *Oscar Wilde*

I should have suspected my husband was lazy. On our wedding day, his mother told me "I'm not losing a son; I'm gaining a couch."
— *Phyllis Diller*

The best way to get most husbands to do something is to suggest that perhaps they're too old to do it.
— *Anne Bancroft*

When a husband brings his wife flowers for no reason, there's a reason.
— *Marian Jordan as Molly McGee, on radio's* Fibber McGee and Molly

When people ask how we've lived past 100, I say "Honey, we were never married. We never had husbands to worry us to death."
— *Bessie Delany, on the secret of her and her sister's long life*

Before marriage, a man declares that he would lay down his life for you; after marriage he won't even lay down his newspaper to talk to you.
— *Helen Rowland*

Ah, my husband is a sort of promissory note; I'm tired of meeting him.
— *Oscar Wilde,* A Woman of No Importance

I was once so poor I didn't know where my next husband was coming from.
— *Mae West*

Husbands are like fires. They go out when unattended.
— *Zsa Zsa Gabor [among others]*

As I've explained to my wife many times, you have to kill your wife or mistress to get on the front page of the papers.
— *Julian Barnes*

There is only one real tragedy in a woman's life. The fact that her past is always her lover, and her future invariably her husband.
— *Oscar Wilde,* An Ideal Husband

The only way a woman can ever reform a man is by boring him so completely that he loses all possible interest in life.
— *Oscar Wilde,* The Picture of Dorian Gray

The nation needs to return to the colonial trend of life, when a wife was judged by the amount of wood she could split, or buckets of coal she could carry up from the cellar.
— *W. C. Fields,* Fields for President

There is an art to "catching a husband": "keeping" him is a profession.
— *Simone de Beauvoir*

A man's mother is his misfortune, but his wife is his fault.
— *Walter Bagehot*

My wife's a hobby-horse…
— *William Shakespeare,* The Winter's Tale

When a woman marries again, it is because she detested her first husband. When a man marries again, it is because he adored his first wife. Women try their luck; men risk theirs.
— *Oscar Wilde,* The Picture of Dorian Gray

A woman worries about the future until she gets a husband, while a man never worries about the future until he gets a wife.
— *Anonymous*

Mary and I have been married 47 years and not once have we ever had an argument serious enough to mention the word "divorce"…"murder," yes, but "divorce," never.
—*Jack Benny*

… a good marriage needs a blind wife and a deaf husband.
—*Michel de Montaigne*

My husband says I treat him like he's a god; every meal is a burnt offering.
—*Rhonda Hansome*

I don't think a prostitute is more moral than a wife, but they are doing the same thing.
—*Prince Philip*

My husband said he needed more space. So I locked him outside.
—*Roseanne Barr*

In my house I'm the boss. My wife is just the decision maker.
—*Woody Allen*

My husband and I divorced over religious differences.
He thought he was God, and I didn't.
   —*Anonymous*

The only good husbands stay bachelors: They're too
considerate to get married.
   —*Finley Peter Dunne*

I give unto my wife my second best bed, with the furniture.
   —*William Shakespeare's will*

A wife…is essential to vast longevity; she is the receptacle of
half a man's cares, and two-thirds of his ill-humor.
   —*Charles Reade,* White Lies

At first a woman doesn't want anything but a husband,
but just as soon as she gets one, she wants everything else in
the world.
   —*Elbert Hubbard*

People shop for a bathing suit with more care than they do a husband or wife. The rules are the same. Look for something you'll feel comfortable wearing. Allow for room to grow.
— *Erma Bombeck*

[The perfect husband] tells you when you've got on too much lipstick and helps you with your girdle when your hips stick.
— *Ogden Nash*

My wife and I had to stop breakfasting together or our marriage would have been wrecked.
— *Winston Churchill*

You only require two things in life: your sanity and your wife.
— *Tony Blair*

It is a truth universally acknowledged, that a single man in possession of a good fortune, must be in want of a wife.
— *Jane Austen,* Pride and Prejudice

All husbands are alike, but they have different faces so you can tell them apart.
— *Ogden Nash*

Being a husband is just like any other job; it's much easier if you like your boss.
— *Anonymous*

He that hath wife and children hath given hostages to fortune; for they are impediments to great enterprises, either of virtue or mischief.
— *Francis Bacon*

I began to think seriously of matrimony, and chose my wife, as she did her wedding gown, not for a fine glossy surface, but such qualities as would wear well.
— *Oliver Goldsmith,* The Vicar of Wakefield

Wives are young men's mistresses, companions for middle age, and old men's nurses.
— *Francis Bacon*

My most brilliant achievement was my ability to persuade my wife to marry me.
— *Winston Churchill*

A husband is a man who two minutes after his head touches the pillow is snoring like an overloaded omnibus.
— *Ogden Nash*

He that displays too often his wife and his wallet is in danger of having both of them borrowed.
— *Benjamin Franklin*

A psychiatrist is a person who will give you expensive answers that your wife will give you for free.
— *Anonymous*

One of the best hearing aids a man can have is an attentive wife.
— *Groucho Marx*

A little House well fill'd, a little Field well till'd, and a little Wife well will'd, are great Riches.
— *Benjamin Franklin,* Poor Richard's Almanack

What a kid I got, I told him about the birds and the bee and he told me about the butcher and my wife.
— *Rodney Dangerfield*

London is full of women who trust their husbands. One can always recognize them. They look so thoroughly unhappy.
— *Oscar Wilde,* Lady Windermere's Fan

Insults

His mother should have thrown him away and kept the stork.
  —*Mae West*

I've had a perfectly wonderful evening—but this wasn't it.
  —*Groucho Marx*

Is your vagina in the New York City guide books? Because it should be; it's the hottest spot in town, it's always open!
  —*Kristin Davis as Charlotte York, on* Sex and the City

I never saw anybody take so long to dress, and with such little result.
  —*Oscar Wilde,* The Importance of Being Earnest

If I had a head like yours, I'd have it circumcised.
  —*Dave Allen*

I have seen more intelligent creatures than you lying on their backs at the bottoms of ponds. I have seen better organized creatures than you running round farmyards with their heads cut off.

—*Connie Booth as Sybil Fawlty, on* Fawlty Towers

She had much in common with Hitler, only no moustache.

—*Noël Coward, of Mary Baker Eddy*

You are, without doubt, the most repulsive individual I have ever met. I would shake your hand but I fear it would come off.

—*Rowan Atkinson as Edmund Blackadder, on* Blackadder

Out of my sight! Thou dost infect my eyes.

—*William Shakespeare,* Richard III

It is absurd to divide people into good and bad. People are either charming or tedious.

—*Oscar Wilde,* Lady Windermere's Fan

I love everything about you. Your lips, your eyes, your voice. The only thing I can't stand is you.

—*Groucho Marx*

Oh, what a pretty dress—and so cheap!
    —*Zsa Zsa Gabor*

[He] must have been a magnificent build before his stomach went in for a career of its own.
    —*Margaret Halsey*

Away, thou issue of a mangy dog!
    —*William Shakespeare,* Timon of Athens

Some men are born mediocre, some men achieve mediocrity, and some men have mediocrity thrust upon them. With Major Major it had been all three.
    —*Joseph Heller,* Catch-22

[He] may look like an idiot and talk like an idiot but don't let that fool you: He really is an idiot.
    —*Groucho Marx, in* Duck Soup

You blocks, you stones, you worse than senseless things!
    —*William Shakespeare,* Julius Caesar

The only decent impression he can do is of a man with no talent.
> —*Rowan Atkinson as Edmund Blackadder,*
> *on* Blackadder

Thinking. Not your strong point, is it?
> —*Heather Graham as Judy Robinson,*
> *in* Lost in Space

Marry me and I'll never look at another horse.
> —*Groucho Marx, in* A Day at the Races

[She was] a perfect saint amongst women, but so dreadfully dowdy that she reminded one of a badly bound hymn-book.
> —*Oscar Wilde,* The Picture of Dorian Gray

What he lacks in intelligence, he makes up for in stupidity.
> —*Anonymous*

I'd call him a sadistic, hippophilic necrophile, but that would be beating a dead horse.
> —*Woody Allen*

Frailty, thy name is woman.
   —William Shakespeare, Hamlet

Most people are other people. Their thoughts are
someone else's opinions, their lives a mimicry, their
passions a quotation.
   —Oscar Wilde, De Profundis

Your mother was a hamster and your father smelt
of elderberries.
   —Frenchman, in Monty Python and the Holy Grail

I never forget a face, but in your case I'll be glad to make
an exception.
   —Groucho Marx

Get you gone, you dwarf;
You minimus, of hindering knot-grass made;
You bead, you acorn.
   —William Shakespeare, A Midsummer Night's
    Dream

...rather like being savaged by a dead sheep.
   —Denis Healey, on being criticized by Geoffrey Howe

We don't have to put up with your snidey remarks, your total slobbiness, your socks that set off the sprinkler system.
—*Chris Barrie as Arnold Rimmer, on* Red Dwarf

God, I hope you're not inviting that bloody, bollocky, selfish, two-faced, chicken, bastard, pig-dog man, are you?
—*Jennifer Saunders as Edina Monsoon,
on* Absolutely Fabulous

There goes a woman who knows all the things that can be taught and none of the things that cannot be taught.
—*Coco Chanel*

Never speak disrespectfully of Society....Only people who can't get into it do that.
—*Oscar Wilde,* The Importance of Being Earnest

Let's at least ask someone who's going to give us a slightly more intelligent opinion. Hello, wall! What do you think?
—*Chloë Annett as Kristine Kochanski, on* Red Dwarf

If there's a mental health organization that raises money for people like you, be sure to let me know.
—*Jack Nicholson as Frank Sachs,
in* As Good as It Gets

He has not so much brain as ear-wax.
  —*William Shakespeare,* Troilus and Cressida

The truckman, the trashman, and the policeman on the
block may call me Alice but you may not.
  —*Alice Roosevelt Longworth,*
    to Senator Joseph McCarthy

I won't eat anything that has intelligent life but I would
gladly eat a network executive or a politician.
  —*Marty Feldman*

People nowadays are so absolutely superficial that they don't
understand the philosophy of the superficial.
  —*Oscar Wilde,* A Woman of No Importance

He hath eaten me out of house and home; he hath put all
my substance into that fat belly of his.
  —*William Shakespeare,* Henry IV, Part 2

He's a well-balanced individual—he has a chip on
each shoulder.
  —*Anonymous*

He is useless on top of the ground; he ought to be under it, inspiring the cabbages.
    — Mark Twain

He is deformed, crooked, old, and sere,
Ill-fac'd, worse-bodied, shapeless everywhere;
Vicious, ungentle, foolish, blunt, unkind,
Stigmatical in making, worse in mind.
    — William Shakespeare, The Comedy of Errors

He left his body to science—and science is contesting the will.
    — David Frost

Out, dunghill!
    — William Shakespeare, King John

I'm not offended by all the dumb blonde jokes because I know I'm not dumb…and I also know I'm not blonde.
    — Dolly Parton

My prayer to God is a very short one: "Oh God, please make my enemies ridiculous." God has granted my wish.
    — Voltaire

I have nothing but confidence in you. And very little of that.
— *Groucho Marx*

He thinks too much: such men are dangerous.
— *William Shakespeare,* Julius Caesar

Why don't you do the world a favor? Pull your lip over your head and swallow.
— *Walter Matthau as Max Goldman, in* Grumpier Old Men

You know, you haven't stopped talking since I came here. You must have been vaccinated with a phonograph needle.
— *Groucho Marx, in* Duck Soup

The common people swarm like summer flies...
— *William Shakespeare,* Henry VI, Part 3

My wife had left me, which was very painful. Then she came back to me, which was excruciating.
— *Kelsey Grammer as Frasier Crane, on* Frasier

What a typical woman you are! You talk sentimentally, and you are thoroughly selfish the whole time.
> —*Oscar Wilde,* A Woman of No Importance

...thou lump of foul deformity...
> —*William Shakespeare,* Richard III

[He has] a brain like Einstein's...dead since 1955.
> —*Gene Perret*

That's strange. I usually get some sign when Lilith is in town—dogs forming into packs, blood weeping down the walls.
> —*David Hyde Pierce as Niles Crane, on* Frasier

After a good dinner one can forgive anybody, even one's own relations.
> —*Oscar Wilde,* A Woman of No Importance

He has all the virtues I dislike and none of the vices I admire.
> —*Winston Churchill*

He can compress the most words into the smallest idea of
any man I ever met.
>—*Abraham Lincoln*

The eyes are open, the mouth moves, but Mr. Brain has long
since departed.
>—*Rowan Atkinson as Edmund Blackadder,*
>*on* Blackadder

[She] can talk brilliantly upon any subject, provided that she
knows nothing about it.
>—*Oscar Wilde,* The American Invasion

He was gotten in drink.
>—*William Shakespeare,* The Merry Wives of Windsor

The best part of him ran down his mother's legs.
>—*Jackie Gleason*

A hundred thousand sperm, and *you* were the fastest?
>—*Jim Hightower*

I treasure every moment that I do not see her.
—*Oscar Levant, on Phyllis Diller*

...her beauty and her brain go not together.
—*William Shakespeare,* Cymbeline

I can always tell when the mother-in-law is coming to stay—
the mice throw themselves on the traps.
—*Les Dawson*

Don't torture yourself....That's my job.
—*Carolyn Jones as Morticia Addams,
on* The Addams Family

The plague of Greece upon thee, thou mongrel beef-witted
lord!
—*William Shakespeare,* Troilus and Cressida

He was so crooked that when he died they had to screw him
into the ground.
—*Bob Hope*

Insults

My bathmat means more to me than you.
> —*Kevin Spacey as Buddy Ackerman, in* Swimming With Sharks

Let's shoot him and put him out of our misery.
> —*Alan Alda as Hawkeye, on* M*A*S*H

Here he comes, swelling like a turkey-cock.
> —*William Shakespeare,* Henry V

He's been called cold, rude, self-centered, arrogant, and egotistical. But that's just his family's opinion.
> —*Bob Monkhouse*

The tartness of his face sours ripe grapes…
> —*William Shakespeare,* Coriolanus

My advice would be if you want to pursue a career in the music business, don't.
> —*Simon Cowell, on* American Idol

Some guy hit my fender, and I told him, "Be fruitful and multiply." But not in those exact words.
— *Woody Allen*

Cecily: This is no time for wearing the shallow mask of manners. When I see a spade I call it a spade.
Gwendolen: I am glad to say that I have never seen a spade. It is obvious that our social spheres have been widely different.
— *Oscar Wilde,* The Importance of Being Earnest

Quiet, will you? The man is trying to be dull. Go ahead, Frank, dull away.
— *Wayne Rogers as Trapper, on* M*A*S*H

He is not only dull himself, he is the cause of dullness in others.
— *Samuel Johnson*

If you had lived 2,000 years ago and sung like that, I think they would have stoned you.
— *Simon Cowell, on* American Idol

I think thou art an ass.
— *William Shakespeare,* The Comedy of Errors

Insults

Really, if the lower orders don't set us a good example, what on earth is the use of them?
> —*Oscar Wilde,* The Importance of Being Earnest

Let's meet as little as we can.
> —*William Shakespeare,* As You Like It

Mirror, mirror on the wall, who's the dumbest of you all?
> —*Anne Robinson*

When they circumcised him, they threw away the wrong bit.
> —*David Lloyd George, of Herbert Samuel*

No woman, plain or pretty, has any common sense at all, sir. Common sense is the privilege of our sex.
> —*Oscar Wilde,* An Ideal Husband

You take the lies out of him, and he'll shrink to the size of your hat; you take the malice out of him, and he'll disappear.
> —*Mark Twain,* Life on the Mississippi

Thou crusty botch of nature...
> —*William Shakespeare,* Troilus and Cressida

He's not unlike Hitler, but without the charm.
 — *Gore Vidal, of William F. Buckley*

He is one of those people who would be enormously improved by death.
 — *Saki (H. H. Munro)*

A man's life is of more value than a woman's. It has larger issues, wider scope, greater ambitions.
 — *Oscar Wilde,* An Ideal Husband

For what you see is but the smallest part
And least proportion of humanity.
 — *William Shakespeare,* Henry VI, Part 1

She was so anally retentive she couldn't sit down for fear of sucking up the furniture.
 — *Joanna Lumley as Patsy Stone,*
 on Absolutely Fabulous

I admire him, I frankly confess it; and when his time comes, I shall buy a piece of the rope for a keepsake.
 — *Mark Twain,* Following the Equator

…woo her, wed her, and bed her, and rid the house of her.
> — *William Shakespeare,* The Taming of the Shrew

I shan't be taking my wife with me to Paris. You don't take a sausage roll to a banquet.
> — *Winston Churchill*

If you're going out of your mind, I suggest you pack light. It's a short trip.
> — *Anne Robinson*

You are as a candle, the better part burnt out.
> — *William Shakespeare,* Henry, IV Part 2

You'll have to excuse my mother; she suffered a slight stroke a few years ago, which rendered her totally annoying.
> — *Bea Arthur as Dorothy, on* The Golden Girls

If his IQ slips any lower, we'll have to water him twice a day.
> — *Molly Ivins, of a local congressman*

Away, you three-inch fool!
> — *William Shakespeare,* The Taming of the Shrew

Lady Caroline: In my young days, Miss Worsley, one never met anyone in society who worked for their living. It was not considered the thing.
Hester: In America those are the people we respect most.
Lady Caroline: I have no doubt of it.
— *Oscar Wilde,* A Woman of No Importance

Good night, Rose. Go to sleep, honey. Pray for brains!
— *Bea Arthur as Dorothy, on* The Golden Girls

Last week I stated this woman was the ugliest woman I had ever seen. I have since been visited by her sister, and now wish to withdraw that statement.
— *Mark Twain*

Thou drone, thou snail, thou slug, thou sot!
— *William Shakespeare,* The Comedy of Errors

She wears her clothes as if they were thrown on her with a pitchfork.
— *Jonathan Swift, in* Polite Conversation

He's so fat, he can be his own running mate.
— *Johnny Carson*

She's a big-hearted girl with hips to match.
> —*Henny Youngman*

Ireland and the Irish

In a study, scientists report that drinking beer can be good for the liver. I'm sorry, did I say "scientists"? I meant "Irish people."
> —*Tina Fey*

These two Irishmen were passing a pub—well, it could happen.
> —*Frank Carson*

Other people have a nationality. The Irish and the Jews have a psychosis.
> —*Brendan Behan,* Richard's Cork Leg

Ireland is the old sow that eats her farrow.
> —*James Joyce,* A Portrait of the Artist as a Young Man

I'm Irish. We think sideways.
> —*Spike Milligan*

The Irish are the niggers of Europe…An' Dubliners are the niggers of Ireland…An' the northside Dubliners are the niggers o' Dublin—Say it loud. I'm black an' I'm proud.
—*Roddy Doyle,* The Commitments

An Englishman thinks seated; a Frenchman, standing; an American, pacing; an Irishman, afterward.
—*Austin O'Malley*

The problem with Ireland is that it's a country full of genius, but with absolutely no talent.
—*Hugh Leonard*

This [the Irish] is one race of people for whom psychoanalysis is of no use whatsoever.
—*Sigmund Freud*

Dublin University contains the cream of Ireland: rich and thick.
—*Samuel Beckett*

The Irish are a fair people; they never speak well of one another.
—*Samuel Johnson*

I reckon no man is thoroughly miserable unless he be condemned to live in Ireland.
    —Jonathan Swift

I showed my appreciation of my native land in the usual Irish way—by getting out of it as soon as I possibly could.
    —George Bernard Shaw

When I die I want to decompose in a barrel of porter and have it served in all the pubs in Dublin.
    —J. P. Donleavy, The Ginger Man

…God help the Irish, if it was raining soup, they'd be out with forks.
    —Brendan Behan, in The Big House

May you be in Heaven a full half hour before the Devil knows you're dead.
    —Irish toast

You know it's summer in Ireland when the rain gets warmer.
    —Hal Roach

Our Irish ancestors believed in magic, prayers, trickery, browbeating and bullying. I think it would be fair to sum that list up as "Irish politics."
—*Flann O'Brien*

Politics is the chloroform of the Irish people, or, rather the hashish.
—*Oliver St. John Gogarty*, As I Was Going Down Sackville Street

Health and a long life to you.
Land without rent to you.
A child every year to you.
And if you can't go to heaven,
May you at least die in Ireland.
—*Irish toast*

The Irish are a very popular race—with themselves.
—*Brendan Behan*

God invented whiskey to prevent the Irish from ruling the world.
—*Irish saying*

...the Irish are not at peace unless they are at war...
   —*George Orwell*

There are many good reasons for drinking,
One has just entered my head.
If a man doesn't drink when he's living,
How in the hell can he drink when he's dead?
   —*Irish toast*

When Irish eyes are smiling, watch your step.
   —*Gerald Kersh*

I know I've got Irish blood because I wake up every day with
a hangover.
   —*Noel Gallagher*

An Irish homosexual is one who prefers women to drink.
   —*Sean O'Faolain*

There are only two kinds of people in the world: The Irish
and those who wish they were.
   —*Irish saying*

The Irish do not want anyone to wish them well; they want everyone to wish their enemies ill.
  —*Harold Nicolson*

I once saw a sign on a lift in Dublin that said: "Please do not use this when it is not working."
  —*Spike Milligan*

Geographically, Ireland is a medium-sized rural island that is slowly but steadily being consumed by sheep.
  —*Dave Barry*

If you put an Irishman on a spit, you can always get another Irishman to baste him.
  —*George Bernard Shaw*

The Irish don't know what they want and are prepared to fight to the death to get it.
  —*Sidney Littlewood*

If you do somebody in Ireland a favor, you make an enemy for life.
  —*Hugh Leonard*

We don't have anything as urgent as *mañana* in Ireland.
—*Stuart Banks*

Italy and Italians

All right, but apart from the sanitation, the medicine,
education, wine, public order, irrigation, roads, a fresh
water system, and public health, what have the Romans
ever done for us?
—*John Cleese as Reg, in* Monty Python's
Life of Brian

In Italy for 30 years under the Borgias they had warfare,
terror, murder, and bloodshed, but they produced
Michelangelo, Leonardo da Vinci, and the Renaissance.
In Switzerland, they had brotherly love; they had 500 years
of democracy and peace, and what did that produce? The
cuckoo clock.
—*Orson Welles, in* The Third Man

When an Italian tells me it's pasta on the plate, I check
under the sauce to make sure. They are the inventors of
the smokescreen.
—*Alex Ferguson*

The trouble with eating Italian food is that five or six days later you're hungry again.
— *George Miller*

The Italians have had 2,000 years to fix up the Forum and just look at the place!
— *P. J. O'Rourke*

Let's be frank, the Italians' technological contribution to humankind stopped with the pizza oven.
— *Bill Bryson,* Neither Here nor There

Italy the home of art and swindling; home of religion and moral rottenness.
— *Mark Twain*

Rome seems to be a great fair of shams, humbugs, and frauds. Religion is its commerce and its wealth, like dung in the Black Forest.
— *Mark Twain*

Rome reminds me of a man who lives by exhibiting to travelers his grandmother's corpse.
— *James Joyce, in letter to his brother Stanislaus*

Kisses

A kiss is a lovely trick designed by nature to stop speech when words become superfluous.
> —*Ingrid Bergman*

A kiss can be a comma, a question mark, or an exclamation point. That's the basic spelling that every woman ought to know.
> —*Mistinguett (Jeanne Bourgeois)*

Everybody winds up kissing the wrong person goodnight.
> —*Andy Warhol*

Alas, poor heart,
That kiss is comfortless
As frozen water to a starved snake.
> —*William Shakespeare,* Titus Andronicus

It's like kissing Hitler.
> —*Tony Curtis, on kissing Marilyn Monroe*

If you are ever in doubt as to whether or not you should kiss a pretty girl, always give her the benefit of the doubt.
— *Thomas Carlyle*

His mouth is a no go area. It was like kissing the Berlin Wall.
— *Helena Bonham Carter, on kissing Woody Allen*

The kiss you take is better than you give;
Therefore, no kiss.
— *William Shakespeare,* Troilus and Cressida

I wasn't kissing her, I was whispering in her mouth.
— *Chico Marx*

I married the first man I ever kissed. When I tell this to my children, they just about throw up.
— *Barbara Bush*

People who throw kisses are mighty hopelessly lazy.
— *Bob Hope*

Women still remember the first kiss after men have forgotten the last.
> —*Remy de Gourmont*

We are all mortal until the first kiss and the second glass of wine.
> —*Eduardo Galeana*

Ugh! I've been kissed by a dog! I have dog germs! Get hot water! Get some disinfectant! Get some iodine!
> —*Lucy Van Pelt, in* Peanuts *by Charles M. Schulz*

Last Words

I don't need bodyguards.
> —*Jimmy Hoffa, a month before he disappeared*

I've never felt better.
> —*Douglas Fairbanks, Sr.*

Am I dying or is this my birthday?
> —*Nancy Astor, seeing her family gathered around her sick bed*

Codeine…bourbon…
> —*Tallulah Bankhead, asked if there was*
> *any final thing she wanted*

I can't sleep.
> —*J. M. Barrie*

It is nothing….It is nothing.
> —*Archduke Franz Ferdinand, after being fatally shot*
> *in Sarajevo in 1914*

Thank you, sister. May you be the mother of a bishop.
> —*Brendan Behan, to nun nursing him*
> *on his deathbed*

My wallpaper and I are fighting a duel to the death. One of
the other of us has to go.
> —*Oscar Wilde*

Now, now, my good man, this is no time for making
new enemies.
> —*Voltaire, asked by a priest to renounce the Devil,*
> *on his deathbed*

Law and Lawyers

The first thing we do, let's kill all the lawyers.
—*William Shakespeare,* King Henry, VI Part 2

I was sued by a woman who claimed that she became pregnant because she watched me on the television and I bent her contraceptive coil.
—*Uri Geller*

The minute you read something and you can't understand it, you can almost be sure that it was drawn up by a lawyer.
—*Will Rogers*

The law is a ass—a idiot.
—*Charles Dickens,* Oliver Twist

A lawyer will do anything to win a case. Sometimes he will even tell the truth.
—*Patrick Murray*

A lawyer with his briefcase can steal more than a hundred men with guns.
　　　—*Mario Puzo,* The Godfather

Litigation, n. A machine which you go into as a pig and come out of as a sausage.
　　　—*Ambrose Bierce,* The Devil's Dictionary

Make crime pay. Become a lawyer.
　　　—*Will Rogers*

It is impossible to obtain a conviction for sodomy from an English jury. Half of them don't believe that it can physically be done, and the other half are doing it.
　　　—*Winston Churchill*

And God said: "Let there be Satan, so people don't blame everything on me. And let there be lawyers, so people don't blame everything on Satan."
　　　—*George Burns*

Life

It's a funny old world—a man is lucky if he gets out of it alive.
> —*W. C. Fields,* You're Telling Me

Life is full of misery, loneliness, and suffering—and it's all over much too soon.
> —*Woody Allen*

All you need in this life is ignorance and confidence, and then success is sure.
> —*Mark Twain*

You fall out of your mother's womb, you crawl across open country under fire, and drop into your grave.
> —*Quentin Crisp*

…life is far too important a thing ever to talk seriously about it.
> —*Oscar Wilde,* Lady Windermere's Fan

[Life] is a tale told by an idiot, full of sound and fury, signifying nothing.
> —*William Shakespeare,* Macbeth

The Answer to the Great Question...Of Life, the Universe and Everything...Is...Forty-two.
> —*Douglas Adams,* The Hitchhiker's Guide to the Galaxy

...life is divided up into the horrible and the miserable.
> —*Woody Allen,* Annie Hall

Life is a sexually transmitted disease and there is a 100 percent mortality rate.
> —*R. D. Laing*

Life is a zoo in a jungle.
> —*Peter De Vries,* The Vale of Laughter

What is human life? The first third a good time; the rest remembering about it.
> —*Mark Twain*

Life was a funny thing that happened to me on the way to
the grave.
 —*Quentin Crisp,* The Naked Civil Servant

If life was fair, Elvis would be alive and all the impersonators
would be dead.
 —*Johnny Carson*

Let us endeavor so to live that when we come to die even
the undertaker will be sorry.
 —*Mark Twain,* Pudd'nhead Wilson

Life is too short for drama and petty things, so kiss slowly,
laugh insanely, love truly, and forgive quickly.
 —*Susan Chapman Melanson and Archie Campbell,*
 Radiation Buddies

Life imitates Art far more than Art imitates Life.
 —*Oscar Wilde,* The Decay of Lying

Life doesn't imitate art, it imitates bad television.
 —*Woody Allen,* Husbands and Wives

Here's to a long life and a merry one
A quick death and an easy one
A pretty girl and an honest one
A cold beer and another one.
  —*Irish toast*

It's possible, you can never know, that the universe exists only for me. If so, it's sure going well for me, I must admit.
  —*Bill Gates*

Life is wasted on the living.
  —*Douglas Adams,* The Restaurant at the End of the Universe

I have a simple philosophy: Fill what's empty. Empty what's full. Scratch where it itches.
  —*Alice Roosevelt Longworth*

My only regret in life is that I'm not someone else.
  —*Woody Allen*

Life is just one damned thing after another.
  —*Elbert Hubbard*

In this world there are only two tragedies. One is not getting what one wants, and the other is getting it.
  — *Oscar Wilde,* Lady Windermere's Fan

When we remember that we are all mad, the mysteries disappear and life stands explained.
  — *Mark Twain,* Notebook

Life is something to do when you can't get to sleep.
  — *Fran Lebowitz,* Metropolitan Life

But sometimes in New York, life is what happens while you're waiting for a table.
  — *Sarah Jessica Parker as Carrie Bradshaw,
    on* Sex and the City

Life is a shit sandwich and every day you take another bite.
  — *Joe Schmidt*

Accept that some days you are the pigeon, and some days you are the statue.
  — *American saying*

All animals, except man, know that the principal business of life is to enjoy it…
— *Samuel Butler,* The Way of All Flesh

Life is a wonderful thing to talk about, or to read about in history books—but it is terrible when one has to live it.
— *Jean Anouilh,* Time Remembered

[Life]…that awkward gap between the cradle and the grave.
— *Alan Bennett,* Getting On

Life is a maze in which we take the wrong turning before we have learnt to walk.
— *Cyril Connolly,* The Unquiet Grave

All the world's a stage, and most of us are desperately unrehearsed.
— *Sean O'Casey*

Life is a moderately good play with a badly written third act.
— *Truman Capote*

The first duty in life is to be as artificial as possible. What the second duty is no one has as yet discovered.
— *Oscar Wilde*

I hope life isn't a big joke, because I don't get it.
— *Jack Handey*

Ducking for apples—change one letter and it's the story of my life.
— *Dorothy Parker*

When I hear somebody sigh, "Life is hard," I am always tempted to ask, "Compared to what?"
— *Sydney Harris*, Majority of One

The four stages of man are infancy, childhood, adolescence, and obsolescence.
— *Art Linkletter*, A Child's Garden of Misinformation

My whole life is a movie. It's just that there are no dissolves. I have to live every agonizing moment of it. My life needs editing.
— *Mort Sahl*

No matter how bad things get, you got to go on living, even if it kills you.
— *Sholom Aleichem*

Experience is the name everyone gives to their mistakes.
— *Oscar Wilde,* Lady Windermere's Fan

Life is not for everyone.
— *Michael O'Donoghue*

Life is a bowl of pits.
— *Rodney Dangerfield*

The trouble with life is that there are so many beautiful women and so little time.
— *John Barrymore*

Life is too short for men to take it seriously.
— *George Bernard Shaw,* Back to Methuselah

Human life is mainly a process of filling in time until the arrival of death, or Santa Claus…
— *Eric Berne,* Games People Play

Half our life is spent trying to find something to do with the time we have rushed through life trying to save.
— *Will Rogers*

My life has a superb cast, but I can't figure out the plot.
— *Ashleigh Brilliant*

The supreme irony of life is that hardly anyone gets out of it alive.
— *Robert Heinlein,* Job: A Comedy of Justice

Everything is dangerous, my dear fellow. If it wasn't so, life wouldn't be worth living.
— *Oscar Wilde,* An Ideal Husband

Life is a near-death experience.
— *George Carlin*

In spite of the cost of living, it's still popular.
— *Kathleen Norris*

Life is what happens to you while you're busy making other plans.
> —*John Lennon [among others]*

When life hands you lemons, make whiskey sours.
> —*W. C. Fields*

Everything has been figured out, except how to live.
> —*Jean-Paul Sartre*

In three words I can sum up everything I've learned about life: it goes on.
> —*Robert Frost*

I find it fascinating that most people plan their vacations with better care than they plan their lives. Perhaps that's because escape is easier than change.
> —*Jim Rohn*

Life is generally something that happens elsewhere.
> —*Alan Bennett*

Life is something that everyone should try at least once.
— *Henry J. Tillman*

"How's life treating you, Norm?"
"Like I just ran over its dog."
— *Coach Pantusso and Norm Peterson, on* Cheers

There is only one immutable law in life—in a gentleman's toilet, incoming traffic has the right of way.
— *Hugh Leonard*

There must be more to life than having everything.
— *Maurice Sendak,* Higglety Pigglety Pop! or
There Must Be More to Life

Life…is like a cup of tea; the more heartily we drink, the sooner we reach the dregs.
— *James Matthew Barrie,* The Admirable Crichton

In the book of life, the answers aren't on the back.
— *Charlie Brown, in* Peanuts *by Charles M. Schulz*

My life is one demd horrid grind.
—*Charles Dickens,* Nicholas Nickleby

The only thing that sustains one through life is the consciousness of the immense inferiority of everybody else, and this is a feeling that I have always cultivated.
—*Oscar Wilde,* The Remarkable Rocket

Were it offered to my choice, I should have no objection to a repetition of the same life from its beginning, only asking the advantages authors have in a second edition to correct some faults in the first.
—*Benjamin Franklin*

Life is like an onion; you peel it off one layer at a time, and sometimes you weep.
—*Carl Sandburg*

Life's tragedy is that we get old too soon and wise too late.
—*Benjamin Franklin*

Life is just a phase you're going through…you'll get over it.
—*Anonymous*

Life is like stepping onto a boat which is about to sail out to
sea and sink.
— *Shunryu Suzuki-roshi*

I think everybody should get rich and famous and do
everything they ever dreamed of so they can see that it's
not the answer.
— *Jim Carrey*

We are born wet, naked, and hungry. Then things get worse.
— *Anonymous*

I am always astonishing myself. It is the only thing that
makes life worth living.
— *Oscar Wilde,* A Woman of No Importance

London

When it's three o'clock in New York, it's still 1938
in London.
— *Bette Midler*

Oh, I love London Society!...It is entirely composed now of beautiful idiots and brilliant lunatics. Just what Society should be.
— *Oscar Wilde,* An Ideal Husband

London is a splendid place to live for those who can get out of it.
— *Lord Balfour of Burleigh*

The truth is, that in London it is always a sickly season. Nobody is healthy in London—nobody can be.
— *Jane Austen,* Emma

[London:] A place you go to get bronchitis.
— *Fran Lebowitz*

When a man is tired of London, he is tired of life; for there is in London all that life can afford.
— *Samuel Johnson*

A person who is tired of London is not necessarily tired of life; it might be that he just can't find a parking place.
— *Paul Theroux,* Sunrise with Seamonsters

London

A man who can dominate a London dinner-table can dominate the world.
> —*Oscar Wilde,* A Woman of No Importance

I don't know what London's coming to—the higher the buildings the lower the morals.
> —*Noël Coward*

And now farewell to London! Dirty little pool of life...
> —*B. M. Malabari,* The Indian Eye on English Life

Can't make out how you stand London Society. The thing has gone to the dogs, a lot of damned nobodies talking about nothing.
> —*Oscar Wilde,* An Ideal Husband

This melancholy London—I sometimes imagine that the souls of the lost are compelled to walk through its streets perpetually. One feels them passing like a whiff of air.
> —*W. B. Yeats*

I'm leaving because the weather is too good. I hate London when it's not raining.
> —*Groucho Marx*

I naturally gravitated to London, that great cesspool into which all the loungers and idlers of the empire are irresistibly drained.

       —*Arthur Conan Doyle,* A Study in Scarlet

Go to London! I guarantee you'll either be mugged or not appreciated. Catch the train to London, stopping at Rejection, Disappointment, Backstabbing Central, and Shattered Dreams Parkway.

       —*Alan Partridge,* I'm Alan Partridge

Love

I was nauseous and tingly all over. I was either in love or I had smallpox.

       —*Woody Allen*

Love, n. A temporary insanity curable by marriage....

       —*Ambrose Bierce*

Love conquers all things—except poverty and toothache.

       —*Mae West*

Love

Do you know what it means to come home at night to a woman who'll give you a little love, a little affection, a little tenderness? It means you're in the wrong house, that's what it means.
  —*Henny Youngman*

Love is blind, but marriage restores its sight.
  —*Georg C. Lichtenberg*

Love is a kind of military service.
  —*Ovid*

Love at first sight is easy to understand; it's when two people have been looking at each other for a lifetime that it becomes a miracle.
  —*Amy Bloom*

Oh, how absurd and delicious it is to be in love with somebody younger than yourself. Everybody should try it—no life can be complete without it.
  —*Barbara Pym*

If it is your time, love will track you down like a cruise missile.
  —*Lynda Barry*

To love oneself is the beginning of a lifelong romance...
— *Oscar Wilde,* An Ideal Husband

Being in love with yourself means never having to say you're got a headache.
— *Ellie Laine*

A guy knows he's in love when he loses interest in his car for a couple of days.
— *Tim Allen*

I've been in love with the same woman for 41 years. If my wife ever finds out, she'll kill me!
— *Henny Youngman*

Some people claim that marriage interferes with romance. There's no doubt about it. Anytime you have a romance, your wife is bound to interfere.
— *Groucho Marx*

I love mankind...It's *people* I can't stand.
— *Linus Van Pelt, in* Peanuts *by Charles M. Schulz*

Love

I was adored once too.
  —*William Shakespeare,* Twelfth Night

I never loved another person the way I loved myself.
  —*Mae West*

But love is not fashionable any more, the poets have killed it. They wrote so much about it that nobody believed them.
  —*Oscar Wilde,* The Remarkable Rocket

The world's tragedy is that men love women, women love children, and children love hamsters.
  —*Joanna Trollope*

My husband and I fell in love at first sight. Maybe I should have taken a second look.
  —*Mia Farrow, in* Crimes and Misdemeanors

Love is an exploding cigar that you willingly smoke.
  —*Lynda Barry*

Love is like war: easy to begin but very hard to stop.
> —*H. L. Mencken, in* Heliogabalus: A Buffoonery
> in Three Acts

If you never want to see a man again, just tell him "I love you. I want to marry you. I want to have children." They leave skid marks.
> —*Rita Rudner*

Every love's the love before in a duller dress.
> —*Dorothy Parker*

Love is not the dying moan of a distant violin—it's the triumphant twang of a bedspring.
> —*S. J. Perelman*

There's only one kind of love that lasts—unrequited love. It stays with you forever.
> —*Woody Allen,* Shadows and Fog

Love is something sent from heaven to worry the hell out of you.
> —*Dolly Parton*

Those who are faithful know only the trivial side of love; it is the faithless who know love's tragedies.
    —*Oscar Wilde,* The Picture of Dorian Gray

Love was only the dirty trick nature played on us to achieve continuation of the species.
    —*W. Somerset Maugham*

I believe in love and marriage, but not necessarily with the same person.
    —*John Travolta*

Love is the delightful interval between meeting a beautiful girl and discovering that she looks like a haddock.
    —*John Barrymore*

Love is a gross exaggeration of the difference between one person and everybody else.
    —*George Bernard Shaw*

True love is like ghosts, which everyone talks about and few have seen.
    —*François de La Rochefoucauld*

Love is like quicksilver in the hand....Leave the fingers open and it stays in the palm. Clutch it, and it darts away.
— *Dorothy Parker*

There is always something ridiculous about the passions of people whom one has ceased to love.
— *Oscar Wilde,* The Picture of Dorian Gray

Love is the child of illusion and the parent of disillusion.
— *Miguel de Unamuno*

Many a man has fallen in love with a girl in a light so dim he would not have chosen a suit by it.
— *Maurice Chevalier, attributed*

Love. Of course, love. Flames for a year, ashes for 30.
— *Giuseppi di Lampedusa,* The Leopard

Love is not merely blind but mentally afflicted...
— *Alice Thomas Ellis*

Love

My wife and I thought we were in love—but it turned out to be benign.
        —*Woody Allen*

Men always want to be a woman's first love...what [women] like is to be a man's last romance.
        —*Oscar Wilde,* A Woman of No Importance

A poll showed that two out of five men would rather have love than money or health. Yeah, that's what a woman wants—a broke, sick guy!
        —*Jay Leno*

If grass can grow through cement, love can find you at every time in your life.
        —*Cher*

Love and scandal are the best sweeteners of tea.
        —*Henry Fielding,* Love in Several Masques

Oh, life is a glorious cycle of song,
A medley of extemporanea;
And love is a thing that can never go wrong;
And I am Marie of Roumania.
        —*Dorothy Parker*

The main purpose of love is to provide a theme for novels.
— *Piers Paul Read*

Carrie Bradshaw: He fell asleep and I watched gay porn.
Samantha Jones: That's what happens when people say "I love you."
— Sex and the City

After all these years, I see that I was mistaken about Eve in the beginning; it is better to live outside the Garden with her than inside without her.
— *Mark Twain*, The Diaries of Adam and Eve

Many a man in love with a dimple makes the mistake of marrying the whole girl.
— *Stephen Leacock*

In love as in sport, the amateur status must be strictly maintained.
— *Robert Graves*

Infatuation is when you think that he's as sexy as Robert Redford, as smart as Henry Kissinger, as noble as Ralph Nader, as funny as Woody Allen, and as athletic as Jimmy Connors. Love is when you realize that he's as sexy as Woody

Love

Allen, as smart as Jimmy Connors, as funny as Ralph Nader, as athletic as Henry Kissinger, and nothing like Robert Redford in any category—but you'll take him anyway.
   —*Judith Viorst*

If love is the answer, could you please rephrase the question?
   —*Lily Tomlin*

Love is like playing checkers. You have to know which man to move.
   —*Jackie "Moms" Mabley*

Love is a game that two can play and both win.
   —*Eva Gabor*

…love, namely the desire of satisfying a voracious appetite with a certain quantity of delicate white human flesh…
   —*Henry Fielding,* Tom Jones

Love is much nicer to be in than an automobile accident, a tight girdle, a higher tax bracket, or a holding pattern over Philadelphia.
   —*Judith Viorst*

For God's sake hold your tongue, and let me love…
— *John Donne, "The Canonization"*

Gravitation cannot be held responsible for people falling in love.
— *Albert Einstein*

[Love] is just a system for getting someone to call you Darling after sex.
— *Julian Barnes, Talking It Over*

No woman is worth more than a fiver unless you're in love with her. Then she is worth all she costs you.
— *W. Somerset Maugham*

Before I met my husband, I'd never fallen in love, though I'd stepped in it a few times.
— *Rita Rudner*

Once in his life, every man is entitled to fall madly in love with a gorgeous redhead.
— *Lucille Ball*

Love

All I really need is love, but a little chocolate now and then doesn't hurt!
    —Lucy Van Pelt, in Peanuts *by Charles M. Schulz*

First love is only a little foolishness and a lot of curiosity.
    —George Bernard Shaw, John Bull's Other Island

I am sick of women who love one. Women who hate one are much more interesting.
    —Oscar Wilde, The Picture of Dorian Gray

Love is a fire. But whether it is going to warm your hearth or burn down your house, you can never tell.
    —Joan Crawford

'Tis brief, my lord…as woman's love.
    —William Shakespeare, Hamlet

Love is the thing that enables a woman to sing while she mops up the floor after her husband has walked across it in his barn boots.
    —Hoosier Farmer

Love is an irresistible desire to be irresistibly desired.
  —*Robert Frost*

Getting divorced just because you don't love a man is almost as silly as getting married just because you do.
  —*Zsa Zsa Gabor*

Forget love—I'd rather fall in chocolate!
  —*Anonymous*

Whatever "in love" means.
  —*Prince Charles, asked if he was in love, after the announcement of his engagement to Lady Diana Spencer*

I had rather hear my dog bark at a crow, than a man swear he loves me.
  —*William Shakespeare,* Much Ado About Nothing

Love is the history of a woman's life; it is but an episode in a man's.
  —*Madame de Staël*

Love

Love is like any other luxury. You have no right to it unless you can afford it.
— *Anthony Trollope,* The Way We Live Now

When one is in love one begins by deceiving one's self. And one ends by deceiving others. That is what the world calls a romance.
— *Oscar Wilde,* A Woman of No Importance

Love is the magician that pulls man out of his own hat.
— *Ben Hecht*

The best love affairs are those we never had.
— *Norman Lindsay,* Bohemians of the Bulletin

Love for me is like a pretzel. Twisted and salty.
— *Emmy Gay*

Love is the delusion that one woman differs from another.
— *H. L. Mencken,* Heliogabalus: A Buffoonery in Three Acts

A man falls in love through his eyes, a woman through her ears.
>   —*Woodrow Wyatt*

The fickleness of the women I love is only equaled by the infernal constancy of the women who love me.
>   —*George Bernard Shaw,* The Philanderer

Love is the triumph of imagination over intelligence.
>   —*H. L. Mencken,* Heliogabalus: A Buffoonery
>   in Three Acts

The people who love only once in their lives are really the shallow people. What they call their loyalty, and their fidelity, I call either the lethargy of custom or their lack of imagination. Faithfulness is to the emotional life what consistency is to the life of the intellect—simply a confession of failure.
>   —*Oscar Wilde,* The Picture of Dorian Gray

Nothing takes the taste out of peanut butter quite like unrequited love.
>   —*Charlie Brown, in* Peanuts *by Charles M. Schulz*

They say love's like the measles—all the worse when it comes late in life.
> —*Douglas William Jerrold,* Time Works Wonders

How alike are the groans of love to those of the dying.
> —*Malcolm Lowry,* Under the Volcano

When love is not madness, it is not love.
> —*Pedro Calderón de la Barca*

Marriage, Cheating, and Divorce

Marriage is a great institution—but I'm not ready for an institution.
> —*Mae West [among others], in* I'm No Angel

A girl must marry for love, and keep on marrying until she finds it.
> —*Zsa Zsa Gabor*

I was married by a judge. I should have asked for a jury.
> —*Groucho Marx*

When you see a married couple coming down the street, the one who is two or three steps ahead is the one that's mad.
　　　—*Helen Rowland*

Marriage is popular because it combines the maximum of temptation with the maximum of opportunity.
　　　—*George Bernard Shaw,* Man and Superman

Your marriage is in trouble if your wife says, "You're only interested in one thing," and you can't remember what it is.
　　　—*Milton Berle*

If we men married the women we deserved, we should have a very bad time of it.
　　　—*Oscar Wilde,* An Ideal Husband

My boyfriend and I broke up. He wanted to get married and I didn't want him to.
　　　—*Rita Rudner*

Egghead weds hourglass.
　　　—Variety *headline on the marriage of*
　　　Arthur Miller and Marilyn Monroe

Marriage, Cheating, and Divorce

Politics doesn't make strange bedfellows. Marriage does.
— *Groucho Marx*

I have always thought that every woman should marry, and no man.
— *Benjamin Disraeli,* Lothair

Marriage is like the witness protection program: you get all new clothes, you live in the suburbs, and you're not allowed to see your friends anymore.
— *Jeremy Hardy*

By all means marry; if you get a good wife, you'll become happy; if you get a bad one, you'll become a philosopher.
— *Socrates*

He's the kind of man a woman would have to marry to get rid of.
— *Mae West*

I am a marvelous housekeeper. Every time I leave a man, I keep his house.
— *Zsa Zsa Gabor*

Marriage is too interesting an experiment to be tried only once or twice.
　　　—*Eva Gabor*

Marriage has no guarantees. If that's what you're looking for, go live with a car battery.
　　　—*Erma Bombeck*

The husband who wants a happy marriage should learn to keep his mouth shut and his checkbook open.
　　　—*Groucho Marx*

I don't believe in extramarital relationships. I think people should mate for life, like pigeons or Catholics.
　　　—*Woody Allen, in* Manhattan

The one charm of marriage is that it makes a life of deception absolutely necessary for both parties.
　　　—*Oscar Wilde,* The Picture of Dorian Gray

A man in love is incomplete until he is married. Then he is finished.
　　　—*Zsa Zsa Gabor*

I love being married. It's so great to find that one special person you want to annoy for the rest of your life.
—*Rita Rudner*

When two people are under the influence of the most violent, most insane, most delusive, and most transient of passions, they are required to swear that they will remain in that excited, abnormal, and exhausting condition continuously until death do them part.
—*George Bernard Shaw,* Getting Married

Marriage, n. The state or condition of a community consisting of a master, a mistress, and two slaves, making in all, two.
—*Ambrose Bierce*

Whatever you may look like, marry a man your own age—as your beauty fades, so will his eyesight.
—*Phyllis Diller*

Marriage to woman is just like jumping through a hole in the ice in winter. You do it once, and you remember it the rest of your life.
—*Maxim Gorky, in* The Lower Depths

Matrimony…no more than a sort of friendship recognized by
the police…
—*Robert Louis Stevenson*, Virginibus Puerisque

Marriage halves our griefs, doubles our joys, and quadruples
our expenses.
—*G. K. Chesterton*

It's a funny thing that when a man hasn't anything on earth
to worry about, he goes off and gets married.
—*Robert Frost*

Dammit, sir, it is your duty to get married. You can't be
always living for pleasure.
—*Oscar Wilde*, An Ideal Husband

Marriage is the alliance of two people, one of whom never
remembers birthdays and the other who never forgets them.
—*Ogden Nash*

Marriage is the only war in which you sleep with the enemy.
—*Anonymous*

The secret of a happy marriage remains a secret.
　　—Henny Youngman

Did you know that 80 percent of the married men cheat in America? The others cheat in Europe.
　　—Jackie Mason

Marriage: A word which should be pronounced "mirage."
　　—Herbert Spencer

An engagement should come on a young girl as a surprise, pleasant or unpleasant, as the case may be.
　　—Oscar Wilde, The Importance of Being Earnest

Never go to bed mad. Stay up and fight.
　　—Phyllis Diller

Bride, n. A woman with a fine prospect of happiness behind her.
　　—Ambrose Bierce

There is nothing nobler or more admirable than when two people who see eye to eye keep house as man and wife, confounding their enemies and delighting their friends.
　　—*Homer,* Odyssey

When a man steals your wife, there is no better revenge than to let him keep her.
　　—*Sacha Guitry*

Getting married is a lot like getting into a tub of hot water. After you get used to it, it ain't so hot.
　　—*Minnie Pearl*

Though women are angels, yet wedlock's the devil.
　　—*Lord Byron*

Divorce: Fission after fusion.
　　—*Rita Mae Brown*

Any intelligent woman who reads the marriage contract, and then goes into it, deserves all the consequences.
　　—*Isadora Duncan*

One should always be in love. That is the reason one should never marry.
— *Oscar Wilde,* A Woman of No Importance

There are good marriages, but no delicious ones.
— *François de La Rochefoucauld*

A bachelor is a selfish, undeserving guy who has cheated some woman out of a divorce.
— *Don Quinn*

To keep your marriage brimming
With love in the loving cup,
Whenever you're wrong, admit it;
Whenever you're right, shut up.
— *Ogden Nash*

Why go out for hamburger when I can have steak at home?
— *Paul Newman, on considering adultery*

In married life three is company and two is none.
— *Oscar Wilde,* The Importance of Being Earnest

For two people in a marriage to live together day after day is unquestionably the one miracle that the Vatican has overlooked.
    —Bill Cosby

Men who have pierced ears are better prepared for marriage. They've experienced pain and bought jewelry.
    —Rita Rudner

It's so long since most married women had sex, they'd probably get motion sickness and would have to tell their partners to pull the bed over to the curb.
    —Kathy Lette

I say, we will have no more marriages.
    —William Shakespeare, Hamlet

[Matrimony]…that high sea for which no compass has as yet been found.
    —Heinrich Heine

No married man is ever attractive except to his wife.
    —Oscar Wilde, The Importance of Being Earnest

Don't marry a man to reform him—that's what reform schools are for.
> —*Mae West*

I've never been married, but I tell people I'm divorced so they won't think something's wrong with me.
> —*Elayne Boosler*

Home life as we understand it is no more natural to us than a cage is natural to a cockatoo.
> —*George Bernard Shaw,* Getting Married

Many a good hanging prevents a bad marriage...
> —*William Shakespeare,* Twelfth Night

Divorces are made in Heaven.
> —*Oscar Wilde,* The Importance of Being Earnest

Take care of him. Make him feel important.... And if you can do that, you'll have a happy and wonderful marriage—like two out of every ten couples.
> —*Neil Simon,* Barefoot in the Park

Why get married and make one man miserable when I can stay single and make thousands miserable?
— *Carrie P. Snow*

Tolerance is the one essential ingredient…You can take it from me that the Queen has the quality of tolerance in abundance.
— *Prince Philip, on his recipe for a happy marriage*

Men are my hobby. If I ever got married, I'd have to give it up.
— *Mae West*

When a girl marries she exchanges the attentions of many men for the inattention of one.
— *Helen Rowland*

Ah yes, divorce comes from the Latin word meaning "to rip out a man's genitals through his wallet."
— *Robin Williams*

Marriage is a bribe to make a housekeeper think she's a householder…
— *Thornton Wilder,* The Merchant of Yonkers

Marriage, Cheating, and Divorce

Women have become so highly educated...that nothing should surprise us nowadays, except happy marriages.
— *Oscar Wilde,* A Woman of No Importance

Men are April when they woo, December when they wed.
— *William Shakespeare,* As You Like It

I'm not upset about my divorce. I'm only upset I'm not a widow.
— *Roseanne Barr, after divorcing Tom Arnold*

All men make mistakes, but married men find out about them sooner.
— *Red Skelton*

Don't get mad, get everything.
— *Ivana Trump, advice to wives whose husbands left them for younger women, in* The First Wives Club

Marriage is but for a little while. It is alimony that is forever.
— *Quentin Crisp*

I was married for 17 years, and I couldn't pick out his face in a police lineup. I can't even remember his face.
—*Joy Behar*

I am not in favor of long engagements. They give people the opportunity of finding out each other's characters before marriage, which I think is never advisable.
—*Oscar Wilde,* The Importance of Being Earnest

After marriage, a woman's sight becomes so keen that she can see right through her husband without looking at him, and a man's so dull that he can look right through his wife without seeing her.
—*Helen Rowland,* A Guide to Men

Why do Jewish divorces cost so much? Because they're worth it.
—*Henny Youngman*

Paying alimony is like feeding hay to a dead horse.
—*Groucho Marx [among others]*

My wife and I are getting remarried. Our divorce didn't work out.
—*Rodney Dangerfield*

Girls never marry the men they flirt with. Girls don't think it right.
> —*Oscar Wilde,* The Importance of Being Earnest

My husband and I had our best sex during our divorce. It was like cheating on our lawyers.
> —*Priscilla Lopez,* Cheaper to Keep Her

A wedding is just like a funeral except that you get to smell your own flowers.
> —*Grace Hansen*

Twenty years of romance make a woman look like a ruin; but twenty years of marriage make her something like a public building.
> —*Oscar Wilde,* A Woman of No Importance

I came from a big family. As a matter of fact, I never got to sleep alone until I was married.
> —*Lewis Grizzard*

The longest sentence you can form with two words is "I do."
> —*H. L. Mencken*

There's a way of transferring funds that is even faster than electronic banking. It's called marriage.
— *James Holt McGavran*

All marriages are happy. It's the living together afterward that causes all the trouble.
— *Raymond Hull*

The real drawback to marriage is that it makes one unselfish. And unselfish people are colorless. They lack individuality.
— *Oscar Wilde*, The Picture of Dorian Gray

It was partially my fault that we got divorced…I tended to place my wife under a pedestal.
— *Woody Allen*

Every time I try to make my marriage more exciting, my wife finds out about it right away.
— *Bob Monkhouse*

Marriage: A legal or religious ceremony by which two persons of the opposite sex solemnly agree to harass and spy on each other for 99 years, or until death do them join.
— *Elbert Hubbard*

The happiness of a married man…depends on the people he has not married.
> —*Oscar Wilde,* A Woman of No Importance

Men marry women with the hope they will never change. Women marry men with the hope they will change. Invariably they are both disappointed.
> —*Albert Einstein*

My grandmother always said, "Don't marry for money… divorce for money."
> —*Wendy Liebman*

It's perfectly scandalous the amount of bachelors who are going about society. There should be a law passed to compel them all to marry within 12 months.
> —*Oscar Wilde,* A Woman of No Importance

Marriage is an adventure, like going to war.
> —*G. K. Chesterton*

Alimony—the ransom that the happy pay to the devil.
> —*H. L. Mencken*

Marriage is like a phone call in the night: first the ring, and then you wake up.
> —*Evelyn Hendrickson*

I never married because there was no need. I have three pets at home which answer the same purpose as a husband. I have a dog that growls every morning, a parrot that swears all afternoon, and a cat that comes home late at night.
> —*Marie Corelli*

Marriage is a wonderful invention—but then again, so is a bicycle repair kit.
> —*Billy Connolly*

My wife got the house, the car, the bank account, and if I marry again and have children, she gets them too.
> —*Woody Allen*

I have often observed that in married households the champagne is rarely of a first-rate brand.
> —*Oscar Wilde,* The Importance of Being Earnest

Marriage is a three-ring circus: engagement ring, wedding ring, and suffering.
> —*Anonymous*

Marriage, Cheating, and Divorce

I've sometimes thought of marrying, but then I've thought again.
> —*Noël Coward*

All men are married women's property. That is the only true definition of what married women's property really is.
> —*Oscar Wilde,* A Woman of No Importance

Marrying a man is like buying something you've been admiring for a long time in a shop window. You may love it when you get it home, but it doesn't always go with everything else in the house.
> —*Jean Kerr*

Wedded be thou to the hags of hell...
> —*William Shakespeare,* Henry VI, Part 2

I've married a few people I shouldn't have, but haven't we all?
> —*Mamie Van Doren*

Men marry because they are tired; women, because they are curious: both are disappointed.
> —*Oscar Wilde,* The Picture of Dorian Gray

Some people ask the secret of our long marriage. We take time to go to a restaurant two times a week. A little candlelight, dinner, soft music, and dancing. She goes Tuesdays, I go Fridays.
> —*Henry Youngman*

They say marriages are made in heaven, but so are thunder and lightning.
> —*Clint Eastwood*

Whenever you want to marry someone, go have lunch with his ex-wife.
> —*Shelley Winters*

Marriage is an alliance entered into by a man who can't sleep with the window shut, and a woman who can't sleep with the window open.
> —*George Bernard Shaw*

The chain of wedlock is so heavy that it takes two to carry it, sometimes three.
> —*Alexandre Dumas, père*

The proper basis for marriage is a mutual misunderstanding.
> —*Oscar Wilde*, Lord Arthur Savile's Crime

I've had diseases that lasted longer than my marriages.
— *Nell Carter*

I can't mate in captivity.
— *Gloria Steinem, on being asked why
she hadn't married*

I had rather be married to a death's head with a bone in
his mouth…
— *William Shakespeare,* The Merchant of Venice

Men, Women,
Battle of the Sexes

Nobody will ever win the battle of the sexes. There's too
much fraternizing with the enemy.
— *Henry Kissinger*

What, sir, would the people of the earth be without women?
…Scarce, sir, almighty scarce.
— *Mark Twain*

Only one man in a thousand is a leader of men—the other 999 follow women.
— *Groucho Marx*

Women represent the triumph of matter over mind, just as men represent the triumph of mind over morals.
— *Oscar Wilde,* The Picture of Dorian Gray

Female, n. One of the opposing, or unfair, sex.
— *Ambrose Bierce*

I like a man who's good, but not too good. The good die young, and I hate a dead one.
— *Mae West*

Women are meant to be loved, not to be understood.
— *Oscar Wilde,* The Sphinx Without a Secret

Meaningful relationships between men and women don't last….There's a chemical in our bodies that makes it so that we all get on each other's nerves sooner or later.
— *Diane Keaton, in* Sleeper

Men are from Mars, women are from Venus.
  —*John Gray*

Men and women, women and men—it will never work.
  —*Erica Jong, in* Fear of Flying

There isn't enough wall space in New York City to hang all of my exes. Let me tell you, a lot of them were hung.
  —*Kim Cattrall as Samantha Jones,*
    on Sex and the City

There's two theories to arguing with a woman. Neither one works.
  —*Will Rogers*

The history of women is the history of the worst form of tyranny the world has ever known. The tyranny of the weak over the strong.
  —*Oscar Wilde,* A Woman of No Importance

Sometimes I wonder if men and women really suit each other. Perhaps they should live next door and just visit now and then.
  —*Katharine Hepburn*

The only females that pursue me are mosquitoes.
　　—*Emo Philips*

Anyone who says he can see through women is missing a lot.
　　—*Groucho Marx*

It's not the men in your life that counts—it's the life in
your men.
　　—*Mae West, in* I'm No Angel

By persistently remaining single, a man converts himself into
a permanent public temptation.
　　—*Oscar Wilde,* The Importance of Being Earnest

Bloody men are like bloody buses—
You wait for about a year
And as soon as one approaches your stop
Two or three others appear.
　　—*Wendy Cope,* Serious Concerns

You have to be very fond of men. Very, very fond. You have
to be very fond of them to love them. Otherwise, they're
simply unbearable.
　　—*Marguerite Duras,* Practicalities

I'm tired, send one of them home.
> —*Mae West, on being told ten men were waiting
> for her in her dressing room*

Women and elephants never forget.
> —*Dorothy Parker*

Whatever women do, they must do twice as well as men to be thought half as good. Luckily, this is not difficult.
> —*Charlotte Whitton*

The great question…which I have never been able to answer, despite my 30 years of research into the feminine soul, is, "What does a woman want?"
> —*Sigmund Freud*

No nice men are good at getting taxis.
> —*Katharine Whitehorn*

Women like silent men. They think they're listening.
> —*Marcel Achard*

There isn't any "New Man." The New Man is the old man, only he whines more.
— *Roseanne Barr*

As long as a woman can look ten years younger than her own daughter, she is perfectly satisfied.
— *Oscar Wilde,* The Picture of Dorian Gray

Behind every great man there is a surprised woman.
— *Maryon Pearson*

Bachelors know more about women than married men. If they didn't they'd be married, too.
— *H. L. Mencken*

I only like two kinds of men—domestic and imported.
— *Mae West*

Girls. You never know what they're going to think.
— *J. D. Salinger,* The Catcher in the Rye

Can you imagine a world without men? No crime and lots of happy fat women.
— *Marion Smith*

You never see a man walking down the street with a woman who has a little pot belly and a bald spot.
— *Elayne Boosler*

A man can be short and dumpy and getting bald but if he has fire, women will like him.
— *Mae West*

All women become like their mothers. That is their tragedy. No man does. That's his.
— *Oscar Wilde,* The Importance of Being Earnest

All women dress like their mothers, that is their tragedy. No man ever does. That is his.
— *Alan Bennett*

Why does a woman work ten years to change a man's habits and then complain that he's not the man she married?
— *Barbra Streisand*

I require only three things of a man. He must be handsome, ruthless, and stupid.
 —*Dorothy Parker*

When I eventually met Mr. Right, I had no idea that his first name was "Always."
 —*Rita Rudner*

My mother said it was simple to keep a man, you must be a maid in the living room, a cook in the kitchen, and a whore in the bedroom. I said I'd hire the other two and take care of the bedroom bit.
 —*Jerry Hall*

There are two dilemmas that rattle the human skull: How do you hang on to someone who won't stay? And how do you get rid of someone who won't go?
 —*Danny DeVito, in* The War of the Roses

Men don't get cellulite. God might just be a man.
 —*Rita Rudner*

A man would prefer to come home to an unmade bed and a happy woman than to a neatly made bed and an angry woman.
  —Marlene Dietrich

A successful man is one who makes more money than a wife can spend. A successful woman is one who can find such a man.
  —Lana Turner

Don't cook. Don't clean. No man is ever going to make love to a woman because she waxed the linoleum. "My God, the floor's immaculate. Lie down, you hot bitch."
  —Joan Rivers

That's the thing about girls. Every time they do something pretty, even if they're not much to look at, or even if they're sort of stupid, you fall half in love with them, and then you never know *where* the hell you are. Girls. Jesus Christ. They can drive you crazy. They really can.
  —J. D. Salinger, The Catcher in the Rye

I'm not denyin' the women are foolish: God Almighty made 'em to match the men.
  —George Eliot, Adam Bede

People say to me, "You're not very feminine." Well, they can just suck my dick.
　　—*Roseanne Barr*

I've been married to a communist and a fascist, and neither of them would take out the garbage.
　　—*Zsa Zsa Gabor*

Why did God put men on earth? Because vibrators can't mow the lawn.
　　—*Anonymous*

Men have a much better time of it than women. For one thing they marry later. For another thing, they die earlier.
　　—*H. L. Mencken*

Men are creatures with two legs and eight hands.
　　—*Jayne Mansfield*

Until Eve arrived, this was a man's world.
　　—*Richard Armour*

Men, Women, Battle of the Sexes

Women complain about sex more than men. Their gripes fall into two major categories: (1) Not enough. (2) Too much.
    —*Ann Landers*

I did everything Fred [Astaire] did, only I did it backwards and in high heels.
    —*Ginger Rogers*

The useless piece of flesh at the end of a penis is called a man.
    —*Jo Brand*

Men seldom make passes
At girls who wear glasses.
    —*Dorothy Parker*

When a woman behaves like a man, why doesn't she behave like a nice man?
    —*Edith Evans*

Between men and women there is no friendship possible. There is passion, enmity, worship, love, but no friendship.
    —*Oscar Wilde,* Lady Windermere's Fan

Men are superior to women. For one thing, men can urinate from a speeding car.
— *Will Durst*

Men play the game; women know the score.
— *Roger Woddis*

Women want men, careers, money, children, friends, luxury, comfort, independence, freedom, respect, love, and a three dollar pantyhose that won't run.
— *Phyllis Diller*

You're not too smart, are you? I like that in a man.
— *Kathleen Turner, in* Body Heat

Guys are like dogs. They keep comin' back. Ladies are like cats. Yell at a cat one time…they're gone.
— *Lenny Bruce*

Women want to loved, to be listened to, to be desired, to be respected, to be needed, to be trusted, and sometimes, just to be held. Men just want tickets for the World Series.
— *Dave Barry*

Men, Women, Battle of the Sexes

The first time Adam had a chance, he laid the blame on women.
>—*Nancy Astor*

Twenty years ago, there were all sorts of words you couldn't say in front of a girl. Nowadays, you can say all the words, but you mustn't say "girl."
>—*Tom Lehrer*

On one issue, at least, men and women agree: they both distrust women.
>—*H. L. Mencken*

Feminism is a wonderful idea—until the car goes wrong.
>—*Nicola Zweig*

I think men talk to women so they can sleep with them and women sleep with men so they can talk to them.
>—*Jay McInerney,* Brightness Falls

The main achievement of the Women's Movement was the right to go Dutch.
>—*Gloria Steinem*

I am all for women's rights—and for their lefts too.
  —*Groucho Marx*

If you women knew what we were really thinking, you'd never stop slapping us.
  —*Larry Miller*

Women now have the right to plant rolled-up dollar bills in the jockstraps of steroid-sodden male strippers.
  —*Howard Ogden*

If you think women are the weaker sex, try pulling the blankets back to your side.
  —*Stuart Turner*

Women have a much better time than men in this world; there are far more things forbidden to them.
  —*Oscar Wilde*

A beer and a bonk are available any time but a chap with his own blow dryer who's also a dab hand with a rag roller is well worth lusting over.
  —*Vanessa Feltz*

I don't hate men. I think men are absolutely fantastic…
as a concept.
  —*Jo Brand*

Women have their faults, men have only two: everything
they say, everything they do.
  —*Anonymous*

A good man doesn't just happen. They have to be created by
us women…
  —*Roseanne Barr*

Men should be like Kleenex: soft, strong, and disposable.
  —*Cher*

I love men, even though they're lying, cheating scumbags.
  —*Gwyneth Paltrow*

The male is a domestic animal which, if treated with
firmness and kindness, can be trained to do most things.
  —*Jilly Cooper*

I want a man who's kind and understanding. Is that too much to ask of a millionaire?
    —*Zsa Zsa Gabor*

A woman needs a man like a fish needs a net.
    —*Cynthia Heimel*

The fastest way to a man's heart is through his chest.
    —*Roseanne Barr*

There are two kinds of women: those who want power in the world, and those who want power in bed.
    —*Jacqueline Kennedy Onassis*

What's the difference between a man and a chimpanzee? One is hairy and smelly and is always scratching his rear. And the other's a chimpanzee.
    —*Anonymous*

A woman will flirt with anybody in the world as long as other people are looking on.
    —*Oscar Wilde*, The Picture of Dorian Gray

There is more difference within the sexes than
between them.
— *Ivy Compton-Burnett,* Mother and Son

A woman's a woman until the day she dies, but a man's a
man only as long as he can.
— *Jackie "Moms" Mabley*

A man in the house is worth two in the street.
— *Mae West, in* Belle of the Nineties

Women have a wonderful instinct about things. They can
discover everything except the obvious.
— *Oscar Wilde,* An Ideal Husband

Ah! the strength of women comes from the fact that
psychology cannot explain us. Men can be analyzed,
women…merely adored.
— *Oscar Wilde,* An Ideal Husband

The chief excitement in a woman's life is spotting women
who are fatter than she is.
— *Helen Rowland*

I have an idea that the phrase "weaker sex" was coined by some woman to disarm some man she was preparing to overwhelm.
    —*Ogden Nash*

Men get laid, but women get screwed.
    —*Quentin Crisp*

The two women exchanged the kind of glance women use when there is no knife handy.
    —*Ellery Queen*

Misogynist: A man who hates women as much as women hate one another.
    —*H. L. Mencken*

God made woman beautiful and foolish; beautiful, that man might love her; and foolish, that she might love him.
    —*Anonymous*

Women might be able to fake orgasms. But men can fake a whole relationship.
    —*Sharon Stone*

Men, Women, Battle of the Sexes

The true man wants two things: danger and play. For that
reason he wants woman, as the most dangerous plaything.
— *Friedrich Nietzsche*

When women are depressed, they eat or go shopping. Men
invade another country. It's a whole different way
of thinking.
— *Elayne Boosler*

A woman without a man is like a fish without a bicycle.
— *Gloria Steinem, attributed*

There's no trust,
No faith, no honesty in men…
— *William Shakespeare,* Romeo and Juliet

I married beneath me—all women do.
— *Nancy Astor*

Sigh no more, ladies, sigh no more,
Men were deceivers ever,
One foot in sea, and one on shore,
To one thing constant never.
— *William Shakespeare,* Much Ado About Nothing

How can a woman be expected to be happy with a man
who insists on treating her as if she were a perfectly normal
human being?
>—*Oscar Wilde,* A Women of No Importance

O God, that I were a man! I would eat his heart in
the marketplace.
>—*William Shakespeare,* Much Ado About Nothing

Men are like a deck of cards. You'll find the occasional king,
but most are jacks.
>—*Laura Swenson*

Men are easy to get but hard to keep.
>—*Mae West*

When Man and Woman die, as Poets sung,
His Heart's the last part moves, her last, the tongue.
>—*Benjamin Franklin,* Poor Richard's Almanack

If women didn't exist, all the money in the world would have
no meaning.
>—*Aristotle Onassis*

Men are what their mothers made them.
 — *Ralph Waldo Emerson*

Be to her virtues very kind;
Be to her faults a little blind…
 — *Matthew Prior, "An English Padlock"*

Beware of the man who denounces women writers; his penis is tiny and cannot spell.
 — *Erica Jong*

We women adore failures. They lean on us.
 — *Oscar Wilde,* A Woman of No Importance

A woman can keep one secret—the secret of her age.
 — *Voltaire*

Heaven hath no rage like love to hatred turned,
Nor hell a fury, like a woman scorned.
 — *William Congreve,* The Mourning Bride

The practice of putting women on pedestals began to die
out when it was discovered that they could give orders better
from there.
— *Betty Grable*

The best way to learn to be a lady is to see how other ladies
do it.
— *Mae West*

Oh, woman, woman, when to ill thy mind
Is bent, all hell contains no fouler fiend.
— *Homer,* Odyssey

Woman was God's second mistake.
— *Friedrich Nietzsche,* The Anti-Christ

Do you not know I am a woman? When I think, I
must speak.
— *William Shakespeare,* As You Like It

Next to the wound, what women make best is the bandage.
— *Jules Barbey d'Aurevilly*

A woman's mind is cleaner than a man's; she changes it more often.
> —*Oliver Herford*

Every woman is wrong until she cries, and then she is right, instantly.
> —*Sam Slick (Thomas Chandler Haliburton)*

The most important thing in a relationship between a man and a woman is that one of them must be good at taking orders.
> —*Linda Festa*

As usual, there is a great woman behind every idiot.
> —*John Lennon*

Woman begins by resisting a man's advances and ends by blocking his retreat.
> —*Oscar Wilde*

The quickest way to know a woman is to go shopping with her.
> —*Marcelene Cox*

Being a woman is a terribly difficult task, since it consists principally in dealing with men.
> —*Joseph Conrad*

Disguise our bondage as we will,
'Tis woman, woman, rules us still.
> —*Thomas Moore*

Macho does not prove mucho.
> —*Zsa Zsa Gabor*

Nothing spoils a romance so much as a sense of humor in the woman....Or the want of it in a man.
> —*Oscar Wilde*, A Woman of No Importance

I love men, not because they are men, but because they are not women.
> —*Queen Christina of Sweden*

Men are mad things.
> —*William Shakespeare*, The Two Noble Kinsmen

You should never try to understand them. Women are pictures. Men are problems. If you want to know what a woman really means—which, by the way, is always a dangerous thing to do—look at her, don't listen to her.
> —*Oscar Wilde,* A Woman of No Importance

It's better to be looked over than overlooked.
> —*Mae West, in* Belle of the Nineties

The only way a woman can ever reform a man is by boring him so completely that he loses all possible interest in life.
> —*Oscar Wilde,* The Picture of Dorian Gray

If a girl looks swell when she meets you, who gives a damn if she's late? Nobody.
> —*J. D. Salinger,* The Catcher in the Rye

And of course a man who is much talked about is always very attractive. One feels there must be something in him after all.
> —*Oscar Wilde,* The Importance of Being Earnest

Is there no manners left among maids?
> —*William Shakespeare,* The Winter's Tale

I hate women because they always know where things are.
—*James Thurber*

Mexico and Mexicans

In addition to oil, beer, tequila, silver, and strawberries, Mexico is the number-one producer of Americans.
—*Argus Hamilton*

Mexico: where life is cheap, death is rich, and the buzzards are never unhappy.
—*Edward Abbey*

Poor Mexico, so far from God and so close to the United States.
—*Porfirio Díaz, attributed*

According to a new geographic literacy study, four out of ten American students couldn't find Iraq on a map. However ten out of ten Mexicans could find the U.S. without a map.
—*Jay Leno*

Thousands of Mexicans gathered in Mexico City to protest high food prices. The protest only lasted an hour, because everyone had to leave for their jobs in Los Angeles.
—*Conan O'Brien*

A country where men despise sex, and live for it.
—*D. H. Lawrence,* The Plumed Serpent

Hell, everything's legal in Mexico. It's the American way.
—*Uncle Jimbo, on* South Park

If you can find a greasier sandwich, you're in Mexico!
—*Krusty the Clown, in* The Simpsons Movie

Money and Business

Goddam money. It always ends up making you blue as hell.
—*J. D. Salinger,* The Catcher in the Rye

Money is better than poverty, if only for financial reasons.
—*Woody Allen*

Money can't buy you happiness, but it does bring a more pleasant form of misery.
—*Spike Milligan*

We don't wake up for less than $10,000 a day.
—*Linda Evangelista*

No one can make a million dollars honestly.
—*William Jennings Bryan*

A rich man is nothing but a poor man with money.
—*W. C. Fields*

I don't like money, actually, but it quiets my nerves.
—*Joe Louis*

If you would know the value of money, go and try to borrow some; for he that goes a borrowing goes a sorrowing.
—*Benjamin Franklin*

The more I see of the moneyed classes, the more I understand the guillotine.
—*George Bernard Shaw*

Money and Business

The secret of business is to know something that nobody else knows.
>—*Aristotle Onassis*

Lack of money is the root of all evil.
>—*George Bernard Shaw,* Man and Superman

Money can't buy happiness, but neither can poverty.
>—*Leo Roston*

Wine maketh merry: but money answereth all things.
>—*The Bible, Ecclesiastes*

Money, it turned out, was exactly like sex, you thought of nothing else if you didn't have it and thought of other things if you did.
>—*James Baldwin*

If you want to know what God thinks of money, just look at the people he gave it to.
>—*Dorothy Parker*

I'm living so far beyond my income that we may almost be said to be living apart.
>—*e. e. cummings*

The only way not to think about money is to have a great deal of it.
>—*Edith Wharton,* The House of Mirth

Money: the poor man's credit card.
>—*Marshal McLuhan*

Save a little money each month and at the end of the year you'll be surprised at how little you have.
>—*Ernest Haskins*

All I ask is a chance to prove that money can't make me happy.
>—*Spike Milligan*

My problem lies in reconciling my gross habits with my net income.
>—*Errol Flynn*

If you can count your money, you don't have a billion dollars.
—*J. Paul Getty*

The safest way to double your money is to fold it over once and put it back in your pocket.
—*Kin Hubbard*

When I was young, I used to think that money was the most important thing in life; now that I am old, I know that it is.
—*Oscar Wilde*

I am opposed to millionaires, but it would be dangerous to offer me the position.
—*Mark Twain,* The American Claimant

If all the economists were laid end to end, they would not reach a conclusion.
—*George Bernard Shaw*

My luck is so bad that if I bought a cemetery, people would stop dying.
—*Ed Furgol*

No matter how rich you become, how famous or powerful, when you die the size of your funeral will still pretty much depend on the weather.
— *Michael Pritchard*

When you don't have any money, the problem is food. When you have money, it's sex. When you have both, it's health.
— *J. P. Donleavy,* The Ginger Man

A banker is a fellow who lends you his umbrella when the sun is shining and wants it back the minute it begins to rain.
— *Mark Twain, attributed*

I worked my way up from nothing to a state of extreme poverty.
— *Groucho Marx*

It is better to have a permanent income than to be fascinating.
— *Oscar Wilde,* The Model Millionaire

Well, whiles I am a beggar, I will rail
And say there is no sin but to be rich;
And being rich, my virtue then shall be
To say there is no vice, but beggary.
— *William Shakespeare,* King John

In the midst of life we are in debt.
— *Ethel Mumford*

My formula for success is rise early, work late, and strike oil.
— *J. Paul Getty*

If you think nobody cares if you're alive, try missing a couple of car payments.
— *Earl Wilson*

I get so tired of listening to one million dollars here, one million dollars there. It's so petty.
— *Imelda Marcos*

[A cynic is] a man who knows the price of everything, and the value of nothing.
— *Oscar Wilde,* Lady Windermere's Fan

Rule Number 1: Never lose money. Rule Number 2: Never forget rule Number 1.
— *Warren Buffett*

October. This is one of the peculiarly dangerous months to speculate in stocks. The others are July, January, September, April, November, May, March, June, December, August and February.
— *Mark Twain,* Pudd'nhead Wilson

If only God would give me some clear sign! Like making a large deposit in my name at a Swiss bank.
— *Woody Allen*

Money isn't everything—but it's a long way ahead of what comes next.
— *Edmund Stockdale*

Making a speech on economics is a lot like pissing down your leg. It may seem hot to you, but it never does to anyone else.
— *Lyndon B. Johnson*

Anyone who lives within their means suffers from a lack of imagination.

  —*Oscar Wilde*

Mendoza: I am a brigand: I live by robbing the rich.
Tanner: I am a gentleman: I live by robbing the poor.

  —*George Bernard Shaw,* Man and Superman

There is only one class in the community that thinks more about money than the rich, and that is the poor.

  —*Oscar Wilde,* The Soul of Man Under Socialism

One must have some occupation nowadays. If I hadn't my debts I shouldn't have anything to think about.

  —*Oscar Wilde,* A Woman of No Importance

Mothers and Fathers

God could not be everywhere and therefore he made mothers.

  —*Jewish proverb*

The older I get, the smarter my father seems to get.
——*Tim Russert*

Mothers are fonder than fathers of their children because they are more certain they are their own.
——*Aristotle*

A man knows when he is growing old because he begins to look like his father.
——*Gabriel García Márquez,*
    Love in the Time of Cholera

When your mother asks, "Do you want a piece of advice?" it is a mere formality. It doesn't matter if you answer yes or no. You're going to get it anyway.
——*Erma Bombeck*

Fatherhood is pretending the present you love most is soap-on-a-rope.
——*Bill Cosby*

By the time a man realizes that maybe his father was right, he usually has a son who thinks he's wrong.
——*Charles Wadsworth*

Arthur: It's times like this I wish I'd listened to my mother.
Ford: Why, what did she say?
Arthur: I don't know. I never listened.
    —*Douglas Adams,* The Hitchhiker's
       Guide to the Galaxy

A man's desire for a son is usually nothing but the wish to
duplicate himself in order that such a remarkable pattern
may not be lost to the world.
    —*Helen Rowland*

It would seem that something which means poverty,
disorder, and violence every single day should be avoided
entirely, but the desire to beget children is a natural urge.
    —*Phyllis Diller*

My mother always told me I wouldn't amount to anything
because I procrastinate. I said, "Just wait."
    —*Judy Tenuta*

I never got along with my dad. When I was a kid, other kids
would come up to me: "My dad can beat up your dad." I'd
go, "When?... He cuts the lawn on Saturdays. Nail him out
there when he's got those Bermuda shorts, red tennis shoes,
and sock garters on."
    —*Bill Hicks*

My mother hated me. Once she took me to an orphanage
and told me to mingle.
—Phyllis Diller

My father had a profound influence on me—he was
a lunatic.
— Spike Milligan

To be a successful father, there's one absolute rule: when
you have a kid, don't look at it for the first two years.
—Ernest Hemingway

My mother had morning sickness *after* I was born.
—Rodney Dangerfield

A suburban mother's role is to deliver children obstetrically
once, and by car forever after.
—Peter De Vries

Her mother was a cultivated woman—she was born in
a greenhouse.
— Spike Milligan

If the new American father feels bewildered and even defeated, let him take comfort from the fact that whatever he does in any fathering situation has a 50 percent chance of being right.
—*Bill Cosby*

Fathers should be neither seen nor heard. That is the only proper basis for family life.
—*Oscar Wilde,* An Ideal Husband

You can hit my father over the head with a chair and he won't wake up, but my mother, all you have to do to my mother is cough somewhere in Siberia and she'll hear you.
—*J. D. Salinger,* The Catcher in the Rye

Music

You just pick a chord, go twang, and you've got music.
—*Sid Vicious*

Hell is full of musical amateurs: music is the brandy of the damned.
—*George Bernard Shaw,* Man and Superman

The man that hath no music in himself,
Nor is not moved with concord of sweet sounds,
Is fit for treasons, stratagems, and spoils…
　　—*William Shakespeare,* The Merchant of Venice

Opera is where a guy gets stabbed in the back, and instead
of dying, he sings.
　　—*Robert Benchley*

Country music is three chords and the truth.
　　—*Harlan Howard*

I don't know anything about music. In my line, you don't
have to.
　　—*Elvis Presley*

All music is folk music. I've never heard no horse sing
a song!
　　—*Louis Armstrong, attributed*

Too many pieces of music finish too long after the end.
　　—*Igor Stravinsky*

Music

You can't possibly hear the last movement of Beethoven's Seventh and go slow.
> —*Oscar Levant, explaining his way out of a speeding ticket*

I hate music—especially when it's played.
> —*Jimmy Durante*

Classical music is the kind we keep hoping will turn into a tune.
> —*Kin Hubbard*

Wagner's music is better than it sounds.
> —*Bill Nye*

If in the afterlife there is not music, we will have to import it.
> —*Doménico Cieri Estrada*

New York

New York now leads the world's great cities in the number of people around whom you shouldn't make a sudden move.
— *David Letterman*

New York, the nation's thyroid gland.
— *Christopher Morley*

The Bronx?
No Thonx!
— *Ogden Nash*

A car is useless in New York, essential everywhere else. The same with good manners.
— *Mignon McLaughlin*

New York Taxi Rules:
1. Driver speaks no English.
2. Driver just got here two days ago from someplace like Senegal.
3. Driver hates you.
— *Dave Barry*

New York

The only real advantage of New York is that all its inhabitants ascend to heaven right after their deaths, having served their full term in hell right on Manhattan Island.
— Barnard Bulletin

There's no room for amateurs, even in crossing the streets.
— *George Segal*

Well, little old Noisyville-on-the-Subway is good enough for me.
— *O. Henry,* Strictly Business

New York is an exciting town where something is happening all the time, most of it unsolved.
— *Johnny Carson*

Hating the [New York] Yankees is as American as pizza pie, unwed mothers, and cheating on your income tax.
— *Mike Royko*

New York is my Lourdes, where I go for spiritual refreshment...a place where you're least likely to be bitten by a wild goat.
— *Brendan Behan*

A person who speaks good English in New York sounds like a foreigner.
> —*Jackie Mason*

[New York is]... not Mecca, it just smells like it.
> —*Neil Simon,* California Suite

I've been a New Yorker for ten years, and the only people who are nice to us turn out to be Moonies.
> —*P. J. O'Rourke*

It's so much better to be a neurotic in New York than in Nashville. There they liked me but they didn't understand me. Here they like me *and* understand me.
> —*Stanley Siegel*

New York City safety rules [include]: Always keep your money and other valuables in a safe place, such as Switzerland.
> —*Dave Barry*

New York is a place where the rich walk, the poor drive Cadillacs, and beggars die of malnutrition with thousands of dollars hidden in their mattresses.
> —*Duke Ellington*

New York is the only city in the world where you can get deliberately run down on the sidewalk by a pedestrian.
— *Russell Baker*

Optimists and Pessimists

We are all in the gutter, but some of us are looking at the stars.
— *Oscar Wilde,* Lady Windermere's Fan

Things are never so bad they can't be made worse.
— *Humphrey Bogart*

[A pessimist is] a man who thinks everybody is as nasty as himself, and hates them for it.
— *George Bernard Shaw,* An Unsocial Socialist

An optimist is a fellow who believes a housefly is looking for a way to get out.
— *George Jean Nathan*

It's snowing still....*And* freezing....However...we haven't
had an earthquake lately.
> —*Eeyore, in* The House at Pooh Corner
> *by A. A. Milne*

I don't consider myself a pessimist at all. I think of a
pessimist as someone who is waiting for it to rain. And I feel
completely soaked to the skin.
> —*Leonard Cohen*

Ah, I suppose it's just the same everywhere—the whole
worl's in a state o' chassis.
> —*Sean O'Casey,* Juno and the Paycock *["chassis" is
> the character's mispronunciation of "chaos"]*

It we see light at the end of the tunnel, It's the light of the
oncoming train.
> —*Robert Lowell,* "Since 1939"

An optimist stays up until midnight to see the New Year in.
A pessimist stays up to make sure the old year leaves.
> —*Bill Vaughan*

Eeyore, the old grey Donkey, stood by the side of the stream, and looked at himself in the water. "Pathetic," he said. "That's what it is. Pathetic."
　　—*A. A. Milne,* Winnie-the-Pooh

Politics, Politicians, and Government

It could probably be shown by facts and figures that there is no distinctly native American criminal class except Congress.
　　—*Mark Twain,* Following the Equator

He knows nothing; and he thinks he knows everything. That points clearly to a political career.
　　—*George Bernard Shaw,* Major Barbara

If a politician isn't doing it to his wife, then he's doing it to his country.
　　—*Amy Grant*

I love a dog. He does nothing for political reasons.
　　—*Will Rogers*

A liberal is a conservative who has been arrested.
— *Tom Wolfe,* The Bonfire of the Vanities

We hang the petty thieves and appoint the great ones to public office.
— *Aesop*

Crime does not pay…as well as politics.
— *Alfred E. Newman*

Being in politics is like being a football coach. You have to be smart enough to understand the game and dumb enough to think it's important.
— *Eugene McCarthy*

I'm not a politician. I've only got one face.
— *Brendan Behan*

A politician…one that would circumvent God.
— *William Shakespeare,* Hamlet

I don't know a lot about politics, but I can recognize a good party man when I see one.
— *Mae West*

Oh my God, the dead have risen and they're voting Republican!
— *Bart Simpson, on* The Simpsons

In politics, if you want anything said, ask a man; if you want anything done, ask a woman.
— *Margaret Thatcher*

An honest man in politics shines more than he would elsewhere.
— *Mark Twain,* A Tramp Abroad

Politics is the art of looking for trouble, finding it whether it exists or not, diagnosing it incorrectly, and applying the wrong remedy.
— *Ernest Benn*

In politics, an absurdity is not a handicap.
— *Napoleon Bonaparte*

If God had wanted us to vote, he would have given
us candidates.
> —*Jay Leno*

The problem with political jokes is that they get elected.
> —*Anonymous*

A government that robs Peter to pay Paul can always depend
on the support of Paul.
> —*George Bernard Shaw,*
> Everybody's Political What's What

A good politician…is quite as unthinkable as an honest
burglar or a virtuous harlot.
> —*H. L. Mencken*

Ninety percent of the politicians give the other ten percent a
bad reputation.
> —*Henry Kissinger*

A politician will do anything to keep his job, even become
a patriot.
> —*William Randolph Hearst*

[A politician needs] the ability to foretell what is going to happen tomorrow, next week, next month, and next year—and to have the ability afterwards to explain why it didn't happen.

    —*Winston Churchill, on qualifications for a politician*

Too bad that all the people who really know how to run the country are busy driving taxi cabs and cutting hair.

    —*George Burns*

Politics is supposed to be the second-oldest profession. I have come to realize that it bears a very close resemblance to the first.

    —*Ronald Reagan*

A politician is a fellow who will lay down your life for his country.

    —*Texas Guinan*

Politics, n. A strife of interests masquerading as a contest of principles. The conduct of public affairs for private advantage.

    —*Ambrose Bierce,* The Devil's Dictionary

Suppose you were an idiot. And suppose you were a member of Congress. But I repeat myself.
—*Mark Twain*

Politicians are like diapers. They both need changing regularly and for the same reason.
—*Anonymous*

Nothing is so admirable in politics as a short memory.
—*John Kenneth Galbraith*

High hopes were once formed of democracy; but democracy means simply the bludgeoning of the people by the people for the people. It has been found out.
—*Oscar Wilde,* The Soul of Man Under Socialism

There cannot be a world crisis next week, my schedule is full.
—*Henry Kissinger*

The art of government is the organization of idolatry.
—*George Bernard Shaw,* Man and Superman

Politics are too serious a matter to be left to the politicians.
— *Charles de Gaulle*

We have fallen upon evil times and the world has waxed very old and wicked. Politics are very corrupt. Children are no longer respectful to their parents.
— *King Naram-Sin of Chaldea, 3800 B.C.; inscription found on an ancient tablet in a Constantinople museum*

Democracy substitutes election by the incompetent many for appointment by the corrupt few.
— *George Bernard Shaw,* Man and Superman

Politics is not a bad profession. If you succeed there are many rewards. If you disgrace yourself you can always write a book.
— *Ronald Reagan*

All animals are equal, but some are more equal than others.
— *George Orwell,* Animal Farm

The function of socialism is to raise suffering to a higher level.
— *Norman Mailer*

Men enter local politics solely as a result of being
unhappily married.
— *C. Northcote Parkinson,* Parkinson's Law

Political language…is designed to make lies sound truthful
and murder respectable, and to give an appearance of
solidity to pure wind.
— *George Orwell*

Politics are almost as exciting as war, and quite as
dangerous. In war you can only be killed once, but in
politics many times.
— *Winston Churchill*

I am whipp'd and scourged with rods,
Nettled, and stung with pismires, when I hear
Of this vile politician.
— *William Shakespeare,* Henry IV, Part 1

I am sure, Lord Illingworth, you don't think that uneducated
people should be allowed to have votes?
— *Oscar Wilde,* A Woman of No Importance

I don't know what people have got against the government—
they've done nothing.
—*Bob Hope*

The intermediate stage between socialism and capitalism
is alcoholism.
—*Norman Brenner*

Politicians are the same all over. They promise to build a
bridge even where there is no river.
—*Nikita Khrushchev*

What this country needs is more unemployed politicians.
—*Edward Langley*

Poor George [Bush], he can't help it—he was born with a
silver foot in his mouth.
—*Ann Richards*

I am a Marxist—of the Groucho tendency.
—*Anonymous*

Let him join our campaign. I'd prefer to have him inside our tent pissing out than outside our tent pissing in.
　　　—*Lyndon B. Johnson*

The cardinal rule of politics—never get caught in bed with a live man or a dead woman.
　　　—*Larry Hagman as J. R. Ewing, on* Dallas

The people have spoken—the bastards.
　　　—*Dick Tuck*

One day the don't-knows will get in, and then where will we be?
　　　—*Spike Milligan*

There's no credit to being a comedian, when you have the whole Government working for you. All you have to do is report the facts. I don't even have to exaggerate.
　　　—*Will Rogers*

I never vote for anyone. I always vote against.
　　　—*W. C. Fields*

He may be a son of a bitch, but he's our son of a bitch.
— *Franklin Roosevelt*

Assassination is the extreme form of censorship.
— *George Bernard Shaw,*
The Shewing-Up of Blanco Posnet

Giving money and power to government is like giving
whiskey and car keys to teenage boys.
— *P. J. O'Rourke,* Parliament of Whores

I've always said that in politics, your enemies can't hurt you,
but your friends will kill you.
— *Ann Richards*

A politician should have three hats. One for throwing into
the ring, one for talking through, and one for pulling rabbits
out of if elected.
— *Carl Sandburg*

Get thee glass eyes;
And, like a scurvy politician, seem
To see the things thou dost not.
— *William Shakespeare,* King Lear

All politics is applesauce.
—*Will Rogers*

Politics would be a helluva good business if it weren't for the goddamned people.
—*Richard M. Nixon*

A professional politician is a professionally dishonorable man. In order to get anywhere near high office he has to make so many compromises and submit to so many humiliations that he becomes indistinguishable from a streetwalker.
—*H. L. Mencken*

Everything is changing. People are taking their comedians seriously and the politicians as a joke...
—*Will Rogers*

I believe in benevolent dictatorships, provided I am the dictator.
—*Richard Branson*

Instead of giving a politician the keys to the city, it might be better to change the locks.
—*Doug Larson*

I always wanted to get into politics, but I was never light enough to make the team.
> —*Art Buchwald*

Politics, n. From the Greek *poly*, meaning "many," and *ticks*, meaning "bloodsucking creatures."
> —*Anonymous*

Proverbs

A deaf husband and a blind wife make the best couple.
> —*French*

In God we trust—all others pay cash.
> —*American*

Man thinks and God laughs.
> —*Yiddish*

One who marries for love alone will have bad days but good nights.
> —*Egyptian*

A wife brings but two good days—her wedding day and death day.
> —*English*

A married man is a caged bird.
> —*Spanish*

When a woman is openly bad she is then at her best.
> —*Latin*

A rich man is never ugly in the eyes of a girl.
> —*French*

Coffee and love taste best when hot.
> —*German*

A person without a smiling face should not open a shop.
> —*Chinese*

If the rich could pay people to die for them, the poor could make a wonderful living.
> —*Yiddish*

He who marries does well, but who remains single
does better.
— *German*

There are only two perfectly good men; one is dead, and the
other unborn.
— *Chinese*

What is bought is cheaper than a gift.
— *Portuguese*

Beware of your friends, not your enemies.
— *Yiddish*

Enjoy yourself. It's later than you think.
— *Chinese*

A man thinks he knows, but a woman knows better.
— *Indian (Hindustani)*

Do not employ handsome servants.
— *Chinese*

Every man knows he will die but no one wants to believe it.
— *Yiddish*

Don't marry for money; you can borrow it cheaper.
— *Scottish*

A loved one has no pimples.
— *African (Kenyan)*

Put the light out, and all women are alike.
— *German*

Of all the 36 alternatives, running away is best.
— *Chinese*

Don't be so much in love that you can't tell when it's raining.
— *African (Malagasy)*

Who has a bad wife, his hell begins on earth.
— *Dutch*

Proverbs

With money in your pocket, you are wise and you are handsome—and you sing well too.
  —*Yiddish*

It's better to fall from a tree and break your back than to fall in love and break your heart.
  —*African*

Marriage is heaven and hell.
  —*German*

Be happy while you're living, for you're a long time dead.
  —*Scottish*

Little children, little sorrows; big children, great sorrows.
  —*Danish*

Life is just a dream, but don't wake me up!
  —*Yiddish*

Who marries for love without money has merry nights and sorry days.
  —*Scottish*

The rich man has more relations than he knows.
  —*French*

A weeping man and a smiling woman are not to be trusted.
  —*Indian (Tamil)*

Marriages are all happy. It's having breakfast together that causes all the trouble.
  —*Irish*

Marry in haste, repent at leisure.
  —*English*

A woman is attractive when she is somebody else's wife.
  —*African (Shona)*

He who loves, loves you with your dirt.
  —*Ugandan*

Pretend you are dead and you will see who really loves you.
  —*African*

Proverbs

It is much easier to take care of a sackful of fleas than a woman.
—German

The woman cries before the wedding and the man after.
—Polish

A father is a banker provided by nature.
—French

Love me, love my dog.
—English

Choose your neighbor before you buy your house.
—African (Hausa)

There's more to marriage than four bare legs in a bed.
—English

Always say no, and you will never be married.
—French

Love is a fair garden, and marriage a field of nettles.
—*Finnish*

Why buy a cow if you can get the milk for free.
—*English [among others]*

Life is the biggest bargain—we get it for nothing.
—*Yiddish*

There is no perfect marriage, for there are no perfect men.
—*French*

There's only one pretty child in the world, and every mother has it.
—*English*

Before you marry keep both eyes open; after marriage shut one.
—*Jamaican*

Marriage is like a beleaguered fortress: those who are outside want to get in, and those inside want to get out.
—*French*

A man is often too young to marry, but a man is never too old to love.
>   —*Finnish*

Love many, trust few, and always paddle your own canoe.
>   —*American*

Every man is a king at home.
>   —*English*

A good husband is healthy and absent.
>   —*Japanese*

Religion and God

God is dead—Nietzsche
Nietzsche is dead—God
>   —*Anonymous graffiti*

I would have made a good Pope.
>   —*Richard M. Nixon*

What if we picked the wrong religion? Every week we're just making God madder and madder?
>—*Homer Simpson, on* The Simpsons

Yes, I rather like this God fellow. He's very theatrical, you know, a pestilence here, a plague there. Omnipotence. Gotta get me some of that.
>—*Stewie Griffin, on* Family Guy

Sir, you are one of the most foul, disgusting, immoral, perverted men that I have ever known. Have you considered a career in the church?
>—*Baby-Eating Bishop of Bath and Wells,*
>*on* Blackadder

Not only is there no God, but try getting a plumber on weekends.
>—*Woody Allen*

As God once said, and I think rightly…
>—*Margaret Thatcher*

I admire the Pope. I have a lot of respect for anyone who can tour without an album.
>—*Rita Rudner*

If there is no God, who pops up the next Kleenex?
—*Art Hoppe*

When a woman gets too old to be attractive to man, she turns to God.
—*Honoré de Balzac*

I'm not a fascist. I'm a priest. Fascists dress up in black and tell people what to do, whereras priests…more drink!
—*Dermot Morgan as Father Ted Crilly, on* Father Ted

A good sermon should be like a woman's skirt: short enough to rouse interest, but long enough to cover the essentials.
—*Ronald Knox*

Most of us spend the first six days of each week sowing wild oats, then we go to church on Sunday and pray for a crop failure.
—*Fred Allen*

There is only one religion, though there are a hundred versions of it.
—*George Bernard Shaw*

What's the big deal about going to some building every Sunday? I mean, isn't God everywhere?
> —*Homer Simpson, on* The Simpsons

Everything that used to be a sin is now a disease.
> —*Bill Maher*

How can I believe in God when just last week I got my tongue caught in the roller of an electric typewriter.
> —*Woody Allen*

Oh! I love God. He's so deliciously evil.
> —*Stewie Griffin, on* Family Guy

If God did not exist, it would be necessary to invent him.
> —*Voltaire*

God is love, but get it in writing.
> —*Gypsy Rose Lee*

When we talk to God, we're praying. When God talks to us, we're schizophrenic.
> —*Lily Tomlin*

When I told the people of Northern Ireland that I was an atheist, a woman in the audience stood up and said, "Yes, but is it the God of the Catholics or the God of the Protestants in whom you don't believe?"
—*Quentin Crisp*

I don't pray because I don't want to bore God.
—*Orson Welles*

If there is no hell, a good many preachers are obtaining money under false pretences.
—*Billy Sunday*

Satan probably wouldn't have talked so big if God had been his wife.
—*P. J. O'Rourke*

I don't believe in an afterlife, although I am bringing a change of underwear.
—*Woody Allen*

Because I'm Jewish, a lot of people ask why I killed Christ. What can I say? It was an accident. It was one of those parties that got out of hand.
—*Lenny Bruce*

Heaven, n. A place where the wicked cease from troubling you with talk of their personal affairs, and the good listen with attention while you expound your own.
  —*Ambrose Bierce,* The Devil's Dictionary

Has anyone noticed that in heaven all the interesting men are missing?
  —*Friedrich Nietzsche*

I do benefits for all religions—I'd hate to blow the hereafter on a technicality.
  —*Bob Hope*

If it turns out that there is a God, I don't think that he's evil. The worst you can say about him is that basically he's an underachiever.
  —*Woody Allen, in* Love and Death

Some people say there is a God. Some people say there is no God. The truth probably lies somewhere between these two statements.
  —*W. B. Yeats*

Puritanism: The haunting fear that someone, somewhere, may be happy.
>—*H. L. Mencken*

I'm really a timid person—I was beaten up by Quakers.
>—*Woody Allen*

I thank God I was raised Catholic, so sex will always be dirty.
>—*John Waters*

Don't you think the Almighty has better things to worry about than where one little guy spends one measly hour of his week?
>—*Homer Simpson, on* The Simpsons

When the missionaries came to Africa, they had the Bible and we [Africans] had the land. They said, "Let us pray." We closed our eyes. When we opened them, we had the Bible and they had the land.
>—*Desmond Tutu*

If Jesus came back today, I think he'd throw up.
>—*Jesse Ventura,* Don't Start the Revolution
>   Without Me

He's not the Messiah, he's a very naughty boy!
— *Terry Jones as Brian's mother, in* Monty Python's
Life of Brian

But who prays for Satan? Who, in eighteen centuries, has
had the common humanity to pray for the one sinner that
needed it most…?
— *Mark Twain*

I'm an atheist…thank God.
— *Dave Allen*

Let me pray to God…The bastard! He doesn't exist.
— *Samuel Beckett,* Endgame

Science and Technology

When a man sits with a pretty girl for an hour, it seems like
a minute. But let him sit on a hot stove for a minute and it's
longer than any hour. That's relativity.
— *Albert Einstein*

When they discover the center of the universe, a lot of people will be disappointed to discover they are not it.
>—*Bernard Bailey*

If it squirms, it's biology. If it stinks, it's chemistry. If it doesn't work, it's physics. And if you can't understand it, it's mathematics.
>—*Magnus Pyke*

It's impossible to travel faster than light, and certainly not desirable, as one's hat keeps blowing off.
>—*Woody Allen,* Side Effects

To err is human but to really foul things up you need a computer.
>—*Paul Ehrlich*

Dontopedalogy is the science of opening your mouth and putting your foot in it, a science which I have practiced for a good many years.
>—*Prince Philip*

Only two things are infinite, the universe and human stupidity, and I'm not sure about the former.
>—*Albert Einstein*

The scientific theory I like best is that the rings of Saturn are composed entirely of lost airline luggage.
> —*Mark Russell*

Interestingly, according to modern astronomers, space is finite. This is a very comforting thought—particularly for people who can never remember where they have left things.
> —*Woody Allen,* The Insanity Defense

If Darwin's theory of evolution was correct, cats would be able to operate a can-opener by now.
> —*Larry Wright*

The Ken Starr report is now posted on the Internet. I'll bet Clinton's glad he put a computer in every classroom.
> —*Jay Leno*

Isn't there any way I can change my DNA, like sitting on the microwave?
> —*Lisa Simpson, on* The Simpsons

A computer once beat me at chess, but it was no match for me at kick boxing.
> —*Emo Philips*

And God said, "Let there be light" and there was light,
but the Electricity Board said He would have to wait until
Thursday to be connected.
— *Spike Milligan*

The trouble with the Internet is that it's replacing
masturbation as a leisure activity.
— *Patrick Murray*

On the Internet, nobody knows you're a dog.
— *Peter Steiner,* New Yorker *cartoon*

Never send a human to do a machine's job.
— *Hugo Weaving as Agent Smith, in* The Matrix

Personally, I don't think there's intelligent life on other
planets. Why should other planets be any different from
this one?
— *Bob Monkhouse*

Oh, there's so much I don't know about astrophysics. I wish
I'd read that book by that wheelchair guy.
— *Homer Simpson, on* The Simpsons

If the universe is expanding, why can't I find a
parking space?
— *Woody Allen*

I would love to change the world, but they won't give me the
source code.
— *Anonymous*

Sex

It's so long since I've had sex, I've forgotten who ties
up whom.
— *Joan Rivers*

Is that a gun in your pocket, or are you just glad to see me?
— *Mae West*

If it wasn't for pickpockets and frisking at airports I'd have
no sex life at all.
— *Rodney Dangerfield*

Sex

Sex between a man and a woman can be wonderful,
provided you get between the right man and the
right woman.
>—*Woody Allen*

Sex is one of the most wholesome, beautiful, and natural
experiences money can buy.
>—*Steve Martin*

The big difference between sex for money and sex for free is
that sex for money usually costs a lot less.
>—*Brendan Behan*

Golf and sex are the only things you can enjoy without doing
either of them very well.
>—*Jimmy Demaret*

When I'm good, I'm very, very good, but when I'm bad,
I'm better.
>—*Mae West, in* I'm No Angel

I think people should be very free with sex—they should
draw the line at goats.
>—*Elton John*

My wife is a sex object. Every time I ask for sex, she objects.
— *Les Dawson*

I'm such a good lover because I practice a lot on my own.
— *Woody Allen*

Young men want to be faithful, and are not; old men want to be faithless, and cannot.
— *Oscar Wilde,* The Picture of Dorian Gray

Contraceptives should be used on every conceivable occasion.
— *Spike Milligan*

A terrible thing happened to me last night again—nothing.
— *Phyllis Diller*

Getting married to get sex is like buying a 747 to get free peanuts.
— *Jeff Foxworthy*

Sex

Bisexuality doubles your chances of a date on a
Saturday night.
> — *Woody Allen*

My best birth control now is just to leave the lights on.
> — *Joan Rivers*

I had the radio on.
> — *Marilyn Monroe, when asked if she really had
> nothing on during a photo shoot*

Oh Lord, give me chastity and continence, but not yet.
> — *St. Augustine*

My love life is terrible. The last time I was inside a woman
was when I visited the Statue of Liberty.
> — *Woody Allen, in* Crimes and Misdemeanors

I'm glad I'm not bisexual. I couldn't stand being rejected by
men as well as women.
> — *Bernard Manning*

I blame my mother for my poor sex life. All she told me was, "the man goes on top and the woman underneath." For three years my husband and I slept on bunk beds.
 —*Joan Rivers*

If sex is such a natural phenomenon, how come there are so many books on how to do it?
 —*Bette Midler*

The total amount of undesired sex endured by women is probably greater in marriage than in prostitution.
 —*Bertrand Russell*

Never pass up the opportunity to have sex or appear on television.
 —*Gore Vidal*

Sex alleviates tension and love causes it.
 —*Woody Allen, in* A Midsummer Night's Sex Comedy

I went to a meeting for premature ejaculators. I left early.
 —*Red Buttons*

Sex

Sex: the thing that takes up the least amount of time and causes the most amount of trouble.
>   —*John Barrymore*

An orgasm a day keeps the doctor away.
>   —*Mae West*

No matter how much cats fight, there always seem to be plenty of kittens.
>   —*Abraham Lincoln*

You know that look women get when they want sex?
Me neither!
>   —*Steve Martin [among others, including Drew Carey]*

Sex is a bad thing because it rumples the clothes.
>   —*Jacqueline Kennedy Onassis*

Remember, if you smoke after sex you're doing it too fast.
>   —*Woody Allen*

There are three sexes—men, women, and clergymen.
>   —*Sydney Smith*

I started out to be a sex fiend, but I couldn't pass
the physical.
   —Robert Mitchum

Sex—the poor man's polo.
   —Clifford Odets

A hard man's good to find—but you'll mostly find
him asleep.
   —Mae West

Familiarity breeds contempt—and children.
   —Mark Twain, Notebook

That [sex] was the most fun I ever had without laughing.
   —Woody Allen, in Annie Hall

Sexual intercourse began
in nineteen sixty-three
(which was rather late for me)—
the end of the *Chatterley* ban
and the Beatles' first LP.
   —Philip Larkin, "Annus Mirabilis"

Sex

An intellectual is a person who has discovered something more interesting than sex.
> —*Aldous Huxley*

I can still enjoy sex at 74—I live at 75, so it's no distance.
> —*Bob Monkhouse*

A girl's legs are her best friends, but even the best of friends must part.
> —*Redd Foxx*

Sex is an emotion in motion.
> —*Mae West*

Don't have sex, man. It leads to kissing and pretty soon you have to start talking to them.
> —*Steve Martin*

Humans are the only animal who can have sex over the phone.
> —*David Letterman*

I prefer women with a past. They're always so damned amusing to talk to.
>   — *Oscar Wilde,* Lady Windermere's Fan

Is sex dirty? Only if it's done right.
>   — *Woody Allen,* Everything You Always Wanted to Know About Sex

I admit, I have a tremendous sex drive. My boyfriend lives 40 miles away.
>   — *Phyllis Diller*

I practice safe sex—I use an airbag.
>   — *Garry Shandling*

[I said] I could make love for eight hours. What I didn't say was that this included four hours of begging and then dinner and a movie.
>   — *Sting*

I'll come and make love to you at five o'clock. If I'm late, start without me.
>   — *Tallulah Bankhead*

I'm a terrible lover. I've actually given a woman an anti-climax.
>   —*Scott Roeben*

It isn't premarital sex if you have no intention of getting married.
>   —*Matt Barry*

Erection is chiefly caused by scuraum, eringoes, cresses, crymon, parsnips, artichokes, turnips, asparagus, candied ginger, acorns bruised to powder and drank in muscadel, scallion, sea shell fish, etc.
>   —Aristotle's Masterpiece, *a sex manual and midwifery book published in 1684; the author is unknown—it was NOT written by Aristotle the Greek philosopher*

The difference between sex and death is, with death you can do it alone and nobody's going to make fun of you.
>   —*Woody Allen*

My girlfriend always laughs during sex—no matter what she's reading.
>   —*Steve Jobs*

Personally, I know nothing about sex because I've always been married.
—*Zsa Zsa Gabor*

Sex appeal is 50 percent what you've got and 50 percent what people think you've got.
—*Sophia Loren*

There are a number of mechanical devices which increase sexual arousal, particularly in women. Chief among these is the Mercedes-Benz 380SL convertible.
—*P. J. O'Rourke*, Modern Manners

Sex is God's joke on human beings.
—*Bette Davis*

Sex is like art. Most of it is pretty bad, and the good stuff is out of your price range.
—*Scott Roeben*

Let's forget the six feet and talk about the seven inches.
—*Mae West, in* Myra Breckinridge

Having sex is like playing bridge. If you don't have a good partner, you'd better have a good hand.
— *Woody Allen*

There's a new medical crisis. Doctors are reporting that many men are having allergic reactions to latex condoms. They say they cause severe swelling. So what's the problem?
— *Phyllis Diller*

What's by far the most popular pastime in America? Autoeroticism, hands down.
— *Scott Roeben*

Women need a reason to have sex. Men just need a place.
— *Billy Crystal*

Virginity breeds mites, much like a cheese.
— *William Shakespeare,* All's Well That Ends Well

Homosexuality is God's way of insuring that the truly gifted aren't burdened with children.
— *Sam Austin*

If you want sex, have an affair. If you want a relationship, buy a dog.
> —*Julia Burchill*

Sex at age 90 is like trying to shoot pool with a rope.
> —*George Burns*

My brain—that's my second favorite organ.
> —*Woody Allen*

When turkeys mate they think of swans.
> —*Johnny Carson*

They say all lovers swear more performance than they are able.
> —*William Shakespeare,* Troilus and Cressida

Pizza is a lot like sex. When it's good, it's really good. When it's bad, it's still pretty good.
> —*Anonymous*

Men like women with a past because they hope history will repeat itself.
> —*Mae West*

It's so tiring, making love with women, it takes forever. I'm too lazy to be a lesbian.
> —*Camille Paglia*

Love without sex is still the most efficient form of hell known to man.
> —*Peter Porter*

The backseat produced the sexual revolution.
> —*Jerry Rubin*

A fast word about oral contraception. I asked a girl to go to bed with me and she said, "No."
> —*Woody Allen*

Condoms should be marketed in three sizes…like olives: jumbo, colossal, and super colossal, so that men don't have to go in and ask for the small.
> —*Barbara Seaman*

Is it not strange that desire should so many years outlive performance?
> —*William Shakespeare,* Henry IV, Part 2

I feel like a million tonight—but one at a time.
> —*Mae West*

If God was a woman she would have made sperm taste like chocolate.
> —*Carrie P. Snow*

The only way to behave to a woman is to make love to her, if she is pretty, and to someone else if she is plain.
> —*Oscar Wilde,* The Importance of Being Earnest

God gave man a penis and a brain, but not enough blood to use both at the same time.
> —*Robin Williams*

Love is the answer—but while you're waiting for the answer, sex raises some pretty good questions.
> —*Woody Allen*

Sex

For women the best aphrodisiacs are words. The G-spot is in the ears. He who looks for it below there is wasting his time.
— *Isabel Allende*

The difference between pornography and erotica is lighting.
— *Gloria Leonard*

What do I know about sex? I'm a married man.
— *Tom Clancy*

His finest hour lasted a minute and a half.
— *Phyllis Diller*

I'm the girl who lost her reputation and never missed it.
— *Mae West*

Of all sexual aberrations, chastity is the strangest.
— *Anatole France*

The only time my wife and I had a simultaneous orgasm was when the judge signed the divorce papers.
— *Woody Allen*

I think that making love is the best form of exercise.
— *Cary Grant*

Sex hasn't been the same since women started enjoying it.
— *Lewis Grizzard*

My wife wants Olympic sex—once every four years.
— *Rodney Dangerfield*

Whoever called it necking was a poor judge of anatomy.
— *Groucho Marx*

I sold the memoirs of my sex life to a publisher—they are
going to make a board game out of it.
— *Woody Allen*

Sex is something I really don't understand too hot. You never
know *where* the hell you are. I keep making up these sex
rules for myself, and then I break them right away.
— *J. D. Salinger,* The Catcher in the Rye

Sex

I love the lines the men use to get us into bed. "Please, I'll only put it in for a minute." What am I, a microwave?
—*Beverly Mickins*

I think that sex is a beautiful thing between two people. Between five it's fantastic.
—*Woody Allen*

In my *mind*, I'm probably the biggest sex maniac you ever saw.
—*J. D. Salinger,* The Catcher in the Rye

Many a woman has a past, but I am told that she has at least a dozen, and that they all fit.
—*Oscar Wilde,* Lady Windermere's Fan

When authorities warn you of the sinfulness of sex, there is an important lesson to be learned. Do not have sex with the authorities.
—*Matt Groening*

The Simpsons' Wisdom

I want to share something with you: the three little sentences that will get you through life. Number 1: Cover for me. Number 2: Oh, good idea, Boss! Number 3: It was like that when I got here.
— *Homer Simpson, on* The Simpsons,
as are following quotes

Bart, with $10,000, we'd be millionaires! We could buy all kinds of useful things like...love!
— *Homer Simpson*

Son, a woman is like a beer. They smell good, they look good, you'd step over your own mother just to get one! But you can't stop at one. You wanna drink another woman!
— *Homer Simpson*

"To Start Press Any Key." Where's the ANY key?
— *Homer Simpson, reading computer manual*

To alcohol! The cause of—and solution to—all of life's problems.
— *Homer Simpson*

I'm going to the backseat of my car with the woman I love, and I won't be back for ten minutes.
— *Homer Simpson*

Ah, beer, my one weakness. My Achilles heel, if you will.
— *Homer Simpson*

I like my beer cold, my TV loud, and my homosexuals flaming.
— *Homer Simpson*

Operator! Give me the number for 911!
— *Homer Simpson*

There's no such thing as a soul. It's just something they made up to scare kids, like the bogeyman or Michael Jackson.
— *Bart Simpson*

Donuts. Is there anything they can't do?
— *Homer Simpson*

Dear Lord, thank You for this microwave bounty, even though we don't deserve it. I mean…our kids are uncontrollable hellions! Pardon my French…but they act like savages! Did You see them at the picnic? Oh, of course You did…You're everywhere, You're omnivorous. Oh Lord! Why did You spite me with this family?
— *Homer Simpson*

Homer: Well, he's got all the money in the world, but there's one thing he can't buy.
Marge: What's that?
Homer: [thinks] A dinosaur.

Ah, good ol' trustworthy beer. My love for you will never die.
— *Homer Simpson*

Let us all bask in television's warm, glowing, warming glow.
— *Homer Simpson*

Ah, sweet pity. Where would my love life be without it?
— *Homer Simpson*

And there's nothing wrong with hitting someone when his back is turned.
> —*Homer Simpson*

Ignore the boy, Lord.
> —*Homer Simpson*

Marge, it takes two to lie. One to lie and one to listen.
> —*Homer Simpson*

Facts are meaningless. You could use facts to prove anything that's even remotely true!
> —*Homer Simpson*

You can't keep blaming yourself. Just blame yourself once, and move on.
> —*Homer Simpson*

Family, religion, friendship...these are the three demons you must slay if you wish to succeed in business.
> —*Mr. Burns*

Smithers: There's a small boy on the grounds.
Mr. Burns: Release the hounds.

You tried your best and you failed miserably. The lesson is
"never try."
  —*Homer Simpson*

Beer. Now there's a temporary solution.
  —*Homer Simpson*

Now Bart, since you broke Grandpa's teeth, he gets to
break yours.
  —*Homer Simpson*

Lisa, if the Bible has taught us nothing else—and it hasn't—
it's that girls should stick to girls' sports, such as hot oil
wrestling and foxy boxing…
  —*Homer Simpson*

Inside every hardened criminal beats the heart of a
ten-year-old boy.
  —*Bart Simpson*

Marge, I'm going to miss you so much. And it's not just the sex. It's also the food preparation.
    —*Homer Simpson*

I'm not normally a praying man, but if you're up there, please save me, Superman!
    —*Homer Simpson*

What good is money if it can't inspire terror in your fellow man?
    —*Mr. Burns*

My mom once said something that really stuck with me. She said, "Homer, you're a big disappointment," and God bless her soul, she was really onto something.
    —*Homer Simpson*

I'm Bart Simpson, who the hell are you?
    —*Bart Simpson*

I'm looking for something in an attack dog. One who likes the sweet gamey tang of human flesh. Hmmm, why here's the fellow....Wiry, fast, firm, proud buttocks. Reminds me of me.
    —*Mr. Burns*

And how is education supposed to make me feel smarter? Besides, every time I learn something new, it pushes some old stuff out of my brain. Remember when I took that home winemaking course, and I forgot how to drive?
　　—*Homer Simpson*

Trying is the first step towards failure.
　　—*Homer Simpson*

What's the point of going out, we're just going to end up back here anyway?
　　—*Homer Simpson*

Aw, Dad, you've done a lot of great things, but you're a very old man, and old people are useless.
　　—*Homer Simpson*

It's not easy to juggle a pregnant wife and a troubled child, but somehow I managed to squeeze in eight hours of TV a day.
　　—*Homer Simpson*

Oh no! What have I done? I smashed open my little boy's piggy bank, and for what? A few measly cents, not even

enough to buy one beer. Wait a minute, lemme count and make sure…
— *Homer Simpson*

I'm not a bad guy! I work hard, and I love my kids. So why should I spend half my Sunday hearing about how I'm going to hell?
— *Homer Simpson*

If you really want something in this life, you have to work for it. Now quiet, they're about to announce the lottery numbers!
— *Homer Simpson*

Remember as far as anyone knows, we're a nice normal family.
— *Homer Simpson*

Kill my boss? Do I dare live out the American dream?
— *Homer Simpson*

Getting out of jury duty is easy. The trick is to say you're prejudiced against all races.
— *Homer Simpson*

When will I learn? The answers to life's problems aren't at the bottom of a bottle, they're on TV!
—*Homer Simpson*

I could crush him like an ant. But it would be too easy. No, revenge is a dish best served cold. I'll bide my time until.... Oh, what the hell, I'll just crush him like an ant.
—*Mr. Burns*

Mom, romance is dead. It was acquired in a hostile takeover by Hallmark and Disney, homogenized, and sold off piece by piece.
—*Lisa Simpson*

All right, let's not panic. I'll make the money by selling one of my livers. I can get by with one.
—*Homer Simpson*

The Bible! Talk about a preachy book! Everybody's a sinner! Except this guy.
—*Homer Simpson*

Oh my God! Space aliens! Don't eat me! I have a wife and kids. Eat them!
—*Homer Simpson*

Television! Teacher, mother, secret lover!
— Homer Simpson

I think Mr. Smithers picked me because of my motivational skills. Everyone says they have to work a lot harder when I'm around!
— Homer Simpson

Sensitive love letters are my speciality: "Dear Baby, Welcome to Dumpsville. Population: You. P.S. I'm gay."
— Homer Simpson

What do we need a psychiatrist for? We know our kid is nuts.
— Homer Simpson

Ah, TV respects me. It laughs with me, not at me!
— Homer Simpson

Bonjour, you cheese-eating surrender monkeys.
— Groundskeeper Willie, as French teacher

THE **2,320** FUNNIEST Quotes

The code of the schoolyard, Marge! The rules that teach a boy to be a man. Let's see. Don't tattle. Always make fun of those different from you. Never say anything, unless you're sure everyone feels exactly the same way you do.

—*Homer Simpson*

Your mother has this crazy idea that gambling is wrong, even though they say it's okay in the Bible.

—*Homer Simpson*

Marge, there's an empty spot I've always had inside me. I tried to fill it with family, religion, community service, but those were dead ends! I think this chair is the answer.

—*Homer Simpson*

Get your haggis right here! Chopped heart and lungs, boiled in a wee sheep's stomach! Tastes as good as it sounds!

—*Groundskeeper Willie*

Prayer—the last refuge of a scoundrel.

—*Lisa Simpson*

I have feelings too—like "My stomach hurts" or "I'm going crazy!"

—*Homer Simpson*

Weaseling out of things is important to learn. It's what separates us from the animals...except the weasel.
—*Homer Simpson*

Lisa, vampires are make-believe, like elves, gremlins, and Eskimos.
—*Homer Simpson*

Son, when you participate in sporting events, it's not whether you win or lose: it's how drunk you get.
—*Homer Simpson*

Fame was like a drug. But what was even more like a drug were the drugs.
—*Homer Simpson*

Stealing? How could you?! Haven't you learned anything from that guy who gives those sermons at church? Captain What's-his-name? We live in a society of laws. Why do you think I took you to all those *Police Academy* movies?
—*Homer Simpson*

This house has quite a long and colorful history. It was built on an ancient Indian burial ground, and was the setting of Satanic rituals, witch-burnings, and five John Denver Christmas specials.
—*Mr. Burns*

Smoking

And a woman is only a woman, but a good cigar is a smoke.
—*Rudyard Kipling, "The Betrothed"*

Smoking...kills you, and if you're killed, you've lost a very important part of your life.
—*Brooke Shields*

Cigarette sales would drop to zero overnight if the warning said, "Cigarettes contain fat."
—*Dave Barry*

I've stopped smoking...I think the cost was a lot of it, and not being able to breathe. I first gave up smoking when I was eight.
—*Dave Allen*

Smoking

If you resolve to give up smoking, drinking, and loving, you don't actually live longer; it just seems longer.
— *Clement Freud*

People are so rude to smokers. You'd think they'd try to be nicer to people who are dying.
— *Roseanne Barr*

I smoke 10 to 15 cigars a day. At my age I have to hold on to something.
— *George Burns*

Asthma doesn't seem to bother me any more unless I'm around cigars or dogs. The thing that would bother me most would be a dog smoking a cigar.
— *Steve Allen*

Smoking is one of the leading causes of statistics.
— *Fletcher Knebel*

A cigarette is the perfect type of a perfect pleasure. It is exquisite, and it leaves one unsatisfied. What more can one want?
— *Oscar Wilde,* The Picture of Dorian Gray

I have made it a rule never to smoke more than one cigar at a time.
— *Mark Twain*

Giving up smoking is easy. I've done it hundreds of times.
— *Anonymous, erroneously attributed to Mark Twain*

I was so horrified when I read about the effects of smoking that I gave up reading.
— *Henny Youngman*

I kissed my first girl and smoked my first cigarette on the same day. I haven't had time for tobacco since.
— *Arturo Toscanini*

Sports

Some people think football [soccer] is a matter of life and death....I can assure them it is much more serious than that.
— *Bill Shankly*

Whoever said, "It's not whether you win or lose that counts," probably lost.
— *Martina Navratilova*

Golf is a good walk spoiled.
— *Mark Twain, attributed*

Losing the Super Bowl is worse than death. With death you don't have to get up next morning.
— *George Allen*

Golf is a game whose aim is to hit a very small ball into an even smaller hole, with weapons singularly ill-designed for the purpose.
— *Winston Churchill*

If at first you don't succeed—so much for skydiving.
— *Anonymous*

Cricket is basically baseball on valium.
— *Robin Williams*

If you watch a game, it's fun. If you play it, it's recreation. If you work at it, it's golf.
— *Bob Hope*

Men forget everything; women remember everything. That's why men need instant replays in sports. They've already forgotten what happened.
— *Rita Rudner*

A sportsman is a man who, every now and then, simply has to get out and kill something.
— *Stephen Leacock*

It's not the size of the dog in the fight, but the size of the fight in the dog!
— *Archie Griffin*

Baseball happens to be a game of cumulative tension, but football, basketball, and hockey are played with hand grenades and machine guns.
— *John Leonard*

Winning isn't everything—it's the only thing.
— *Vince Lombardi*

Sports

The sport of choice for the urban poor is basketball. The sport of choice for maintenance level employees is bowling. The sport of choice for front-line workers is football. The sport of choice for supervisors is baseball. The sport of choice for middle management is tennis. The sport of choice for corporate officers is golf. Conclusion: The higher you go in the corporate structure, the smaller your balls become.
    —*Anonymous*

Victory is fleeting. Losing is forever.
    —*Billie Jean King*

Hockey is a sport for white men. Basketball is a sport for black men. Golf is a sport for white men dressed like black pimps.
    —*Tiger Woods*

One should always play fairly…when one has the winning cards.
    —*Oscar Wilde,* An Ideal Husband

I guess there is nothing that will get your mind off everything like golf. I have never been depressed enough to take up the game, but they say you get so sore at yourself you forget to hate your enemies.
    —*Will Rogers*

It's not whether you win or lose—but whether I win or lose!
　　—*Sandy Lyle*

One day of practice is like [just] one day of clean living. It doesn't do you any good.
　　—*Abe Lemons*

If winning isn't everything, why do they keep score?
　　—*Vince Lombardi*

The more I practice, the luckier I get.
　　—*Gary Player*

Baseball has the great advantage over cricket of being sooner ended.
　　—*George Bernard Shaw*

If a man watches three football games in a row, he should be declared legally dead.
　　—*Erma Bombeck*

Rugby is a beastly game played by gentlemen. Soccer is a gentlemen's game played by beasts. Football is a beastly game played by beasts.
— *Henry Blaha*

God, as some cynic has said, is always on the side which has the best football coach.
— *Heywood Broun*

When I played pro football, I never set out to hurt anyone deliberately—unless it was, you know, important, like a league game or something.
— *Dick Butkus*

Pro football is like nuclear warfare. There are no winners, only survivors.
— *Frank Gifford*

Gentlemen, it is better to have died a small boy than to fumble this football.
— *John Heisman*

Football is easy if you're crazy as hell.
— *Bo Jackson*

Jerry Ford is a nice guy, but he played too much football with his helmet off.
—*Lyndon B. Johnson*

He's fair. He treats us all alike—like dogs.
—*Henry Jordan, on football coach Vince Lombardi*

Football players, like prostitutes, are in the business of ruining their bodies for the pleasure of strangers.
—*Merle Kessler*

Football isn't a contact sport; it's a collision sport. Dancing is a contact sport.
—*Vince Lombardi*

Watching football is like watching pornography. There's plenty of action, and I can't take my eyes off it, but when it's over, I wonder why the hell I spent an afternoon doing it.
—*Luke Salisbury*

There are two kinds of people in the world, Notre Dame lovers and Notre Dame haters. And, quite frankly, they're both a pain in the ass.
—*Dan Devine*

Let's face it. You have to have a certain recessive gene that has a little something to do with the brain to go out on the football field and beat your head against other human beings on a daily basis.

— *Tim Green*

Wrestling is ballet with violence.

— *Jesse Ventura*

Baseball is 90% mental and the other half is physical.

— *Yogi Berra*

In a way an umpire is like a woman. He makes quick decisions, never reverses them, and doesn't think you're safe when you're out.

— *Larry Goetz*

Baseball is very big with my people. It figures. It's the only way we can get to shake a bat at a white man without starting a riot.

— *Dick Gregory*

Never hit a man with glasses. Hit him with a baseball bat.

— *Anonymous*

If it weren't for baseball, many kids wouldn't know what a millionaire looked like.
>   —*Phyllis Diller*

It ain't over 'til it's over.
>   —*Yogi Berra*

People ask me what I do in winter when there's no baseball. I'll tell you what I do. I stare out the window and wait for spring.
>   —*Rogers Hornsby*

The last words to the "Star Spangled Banner?" "Play ball!"
>   —*Anonymous*

There are three things in my life which I really love: God, my family, and baseball. The only problem—once baseball season starts, I change the order around a bit.
>   —*Al Gallagher*

For the parent of a Little Leaguer, a baseball game is simply a nervous breakdown divided into nine innings.
>   —*Earl Wilson*

Any American boy can be a basketball star if he grows up, up, up.
> — *Bill Vaughn*

[Basketball] is the second most exciting indoor sport, and the other one shouldn't have spectators.
> — *Dick Vertleib*

If the NBA were on channel 5 and a bunch of frogs making love was on channel 4, I'd watch the frogs even if they were coming in fuzzy.
> — *Bobby Knight*

Giving Magic the basketball is like giving Hitler an army, Jesse James a gang, or Genghis Khan a horse. Devastation. Havoc.
> — *Jim Murray, on Magic Johnson*

What is so fascinating about a group of pituitary cases trying to stuff the ball through a hoop?
> — *Diane Keaton on basketball, in* Annie Hall

When I went to Catholic high school in Philadelphia, we just had one coach for football and basketball. He took all of us who turned out and had us run through a forest. The ones who ran into the trees went on the football team.
—*George Raveling*

I'm sure sex wouldn't be so rewarding as this World Cup. It's not that sex isn't good but the World Cup is every four years and sex is not.
—*Ronaldo, after winning 2002 World Cup*

If you are first, you are first. If you are second, you are nothing.
—*Bill Shankly*

Golf and sex are the only things you can enjoy without being any good at them.
—*Jimmy Demaret*

They call it golf because all of the other four-letter names were taken.
—*Ray Floyd*

Golf is a fascinating game. It has taken me nearly 40 years to discover I can't play it.
— *Ted Ray*

The average golfer's handicap is his IQ. Girls, believe me, if your hubby keeps golfing, he will soon have the brain frequency of a lower primate.
— *Kathy Lette*

Have you ever noticed what golf spells backwards?
— *Al Boliska*

Golf is not a sport. Golf is men in ugly pants walking.
— *Rosie O'Donnell*

I'm not saying my golf game went bad, but if I grew tomatoes, they'd come up sliced.
— *Lee Trevino*

On a recent survey, 80 percent of golfers admitted cheating. The other 20 percent lied.
— *Bruce Lansky*

If profanity had an influence on the flight of the ball, the game of golf would be played far better than it is.

—*Horace G. Hutchinson*

Golf is the most fun you can have without taking your clothes off.

—*Chi Chi Rodriguez*

Show me a man who is a good loser and I'll show you a man who is playing golf with his boss.

—*Jim Murray*

When I die, bury me on the golf course so my husband will visit.

—*Anonymous*

Give me golf clubs, fresh air and a beautiful partner—and you can keep the golf clubs and fresh air.

—*Jack Benny*

Golf is the cruelest of sports. Like life, it's unfair. It's a harlot. A trollop. It leads you on. It never lives up to its promises....[It's] a boulevard of broken dreams. It plays with men. And runs off with the butcher.

—*Jim Murray*

Sports

Tennis is a perfect combination of violent action taking place in an atmosphere of total tranquility. My heart pounds, my eyes get damp, and my ears feel like they're wiggling, but it's also just totally peaceful…
> —*Billie Jean King*

Don't marry a tennis player—love means nothing to them.
> —*Joan Rivers*

Tennis: a racquet sport in which two players compete to see who has the shortest temper, the worst memory, the poorest eyesight, and the slowest watch.
> —*Anonymous*

I am the astronaut of boxing. Joe Louis and Dempsey were just jet pilots. I'm in a world of my own.
> —*Muhammad Ali*

To me, boxing is like a ballet, except there's no music, no choreography, and the dancers hit each other.
> —*Jack Handy*

Boxing is a lot of white men watching two black men beat each other up.
> —*Muhammad Ali*

And I love kick boxing. It's a lot of fun. It gives you a lot of confidence when you can kick somebody in the head.
—*Alicia Keys*

It's just a job. Grass grows, birds fly, waves pound the sand. I beat people up.
—*Muhammad Ali*

Boxing is the only sport you can get your brain shook, your money took, and your name in the undertaker book.
—*Joe Frazier*

I want to rip out his heart and feed it to him. I want to kill people. I want to rip their stomachs out and eat their children.
—*Mike Tyson*

Boxing is just show business with blood.
—*Frank Bruno*

I'll beat him so bad he'll need a shoehorn to put his hat on.
—*Muhammad Ali*

I want to keep fighting because it is the only thing that keeps me out of the hamburger joints. If I don't fight, I'll eat this planet.
— *George Foreman*

I tend to think that cricket is the greatest thing that God ever created on earth—certainly greater than sex, although sex isn't too bad either.
— *Harold Pinter*

Rugby is great. The players don't wear helmets or padding; they just beat the living daylights out of each other and then go for a beer. I love that.
— *Joe Theismann*

Modern rugby players like to get their retaliation in first.
— *Kim Fletcher*

Rugby is a good occasion for keeping 30 bullies far from the city.
— *Oscar Wilde*

I prefer rugby to soccer. I enjoy the violence in rugby, except when they start biting each other's ears off.
—*Elizabeth Taylor*

Rugby is played by men with odd-shaped balls.
—*Anonymous*

I once dated a famous Aussie rugby player who treated me just like a football: made a pass, played footsie, then dropped me as soon as he'd scored.
—*Kathy Lette*

What do you call a cyclist who doesn't wear a helmet? An organ donor.
—*David Perry*

Hockey's the only place where a guy can go nowadays and watch two white guys fight.
—*Frank Deford*

[Ice hockey is] a fast body-contact game played by men with clubs in their hands and knives laced to their feet.
—*Paul Gallico*

Red ice sells hockey tickets.
    —*Bob Stewart*

Half the game is mental; the other half is being mental.
    —*Jim McKenny, on hockey*

By the age of 18, the average American has witnessed 200,000 acts of violence on television, most of them occurring during Game 1 of the NHL playoff series.
    —*Steve Rushin*

Hockey is figure skating in a war zone.
    —*Anonymous*

Hockey is murder on ice.
    —*Jim Murray*

Hockey players wear numbers because you can't always identify the body with dental records.
    —*Anonymous*

Four out of five dentists surveyed recommended
playing hockey.
— *Anonymous*

I love those hockey moms. You know the difference between
a hockey mom and a pit bull? Lipstick.
— *Sarah Palin*

Give blood. Play hockey.
— *Anonymous*

When hell freezes over, I'll play hockey there too.
— *Anonymous*

Swimming isn't a sport. Swimming is a way to keep
from drowning.
— *George Carlin*

Doctors and scientists said that breaking the four-minute
mile was impossible, that one would die in the attempt.
Thus, when I got up from the track after collapsing at the
finish line, I figured I was dead.
— *Roger Bannister*

Can you believe Lance Armstrong? Just 48 hours after
winning the Tour de France he won another race in Austria.
I take the garbage out and I'm pooped for a week.
—*Jay Leno*

Success

If a first you don't succeed, try, try again. Then quit. No use
being a damn fool about it.
—*W. C. Fields*

Eighty percent of success is showing up.
—*Woody Allen*

The penalty for success is to be bored by the people who
used to snub you.
—*Nancy Astor*

Success, n. The one unpardonable sin against one's fellows.
—*Ambrose Bierce,* The Devil's Dictionary

Don't confuse fame with success. Madonna is one; Helen Keller is the other.
>   —*Erma Bombeck*

It takes 20 years to become an overnight success.
>   —*Eddie Cantor*

Success is going from failure to failure without losing your enthusiasm.
>   —*Winston Churchill*

I don't know the key to success, but the key to failure is trying to please everybody.
>   —*Bill Cosby*

If at first you don't succeed, failure may be your style.
>   —*Quentin Crisp*

He was a self-made man who owed his lack of success to nobody.
>   —*Joseph Heller,* Catch-22

Success

It is not sufficient that I succeed—all others must fail.
  —*Genghis Khan*

The worst part of having success is trying to find someone
who is happy for you.
  —*Bette Midler*

The secret to success is to offend the greatest number
of people.
  —*George Bernard Shaw*

Success is a great deodorant. It takes away all your
past smells.
  —*Elizabeth Taylor*

The road to success is always under construction.
  —*Lily Tomlin*

Television

I must say I find television very educational. The minute somebody turns it on, I go into the library and read a good book.
> —*Groucho Marx*

Television has brought back murder into the home—where it belongs.
> —*Alfred Hitchcock*

Why should people go out and pay to see bad movies when they can stay at home and see bad television for nothing.
> —*Samuel Goldwyn*

Before deciding to retire, stay home for a week and watch the daytime TV shows.
> —*Bill Copeland*

Television is a device that permits people who haven't anything to do to watch people who can't do anything.
> —*Fred Allen*

Television

Radio is the theater of the mind; television is the theater of the mindless.
—*Steve Allen*

If you're not on television, you're not an American. All Americans want to be on television.
—*Russell Baker*

Nothing is really real unless it happens on television.
—*Daniel J. Boorstin*

Television is an invention that permits you to be entertained in your living room by people you wouldn't have in your home.
—*David Frost*

TV is simply a place where people go when they get tired of thinking.
—*Kevin Devitte*

Television is for appearing on—not for looking at.
—*Noël Coward*

My father hated radio and could not wait for television to be invented so he could hate that too.
— *Peter De Vries*

Television has raised writing to a new low.
— *Samuel Goldwyn*

I hate television. I hate it as much as peanuts. But I can't stop eating peanuts.
— *Orson Welles*

Television has made dictatorship impossible, but democracy unbearable.
— *Shimon Peres*

[Television] is a medium of entertainment which permits millions of people to listen to the same joke at the same time, and yet remain lonesome.
— *T. S. Eliot*

Television

Television is not the truth! Television is a goddamned amusement park! Television is a circus, a traveling troupe of acrobats and storytellers…sideshow freaks and football players!…We're in the boredom killing business! So if you want the truth, go to God! Go to your gurus! Go to yourselves! Because that's the only place you're ever going to find any real truth. You're never going to get any truth from us. We'll tell you anything you want to hear; we lie like hell…We deal in illusions, man! None of it is true!
    —*Peter Finch as Howard Beale, in* Network

It's television, you see. If you are not on the thing every week, the public think you are either dead or deported.
    —*Frankie Howerd*

American people don't believe anything until they see it on television.
    —*Richard M. Nixon*

It's just hard not to listen to TV: it's spent so much more time raising us than you have.
    —*Bart Simpson, to his dad Homer, on* The Simpsons

I'm delighted with [television], because it used to be that films were the lowest form of art. Now we're got something to look down on.
— *Billy Wilder*

Television? The word is half Greek, half Latin. No good can come of it.
— *C. P. Scott*

You're beginning to think that the tube is reality and that your own lives are unreal! You do whatever the tube tells you. You dress like the tube, you eat like the tube, you raise your children like the tube, you even think like the tube! This is mass madness, you maniacs! In God's name, you people are the real thing. We are the illusion!
— *Peter Finch as Howard Beale, in* Network

Some television programs are so much chewing gum for the eyes.
— *John Mason Brown, attributed*

Sex on television can't hurt you—unless you fall off.
— *Anonymous*

Television has done much for psychiatry by spreading information about it, as well as contributing to the need for it.

—*Alfred Hitchcock*

Thanksgiving

I celebrated Thanksgiving in an old-fashioned way. I invited everyone in my neighborhood to my house, we had an enormous feast, and then I killed them and took their land.

—*Jon Stewart*

I love Thanksgiving turkey—it's the only time in Los Angeles that you see natural breasts.

—*Arnold Schwarzenegger*

Here's a Thanksgiving tip. Generally, your turkey is not cooked enough if it passes you the cranberry sauce.

—*Joan Rivers*

Turkey, n. A large bird whose flesh when eaten on certain religious anniversaries has the peculiar property of attesting piety and gratitude. Incidentally, it is pretty good eating.

—*Ambrose Bierce*, The Devil's Dictionary

May your stuffing be tasty, may your turkey be plump,
May your potatoes and gravy have nary a lump.
May your yams be delicious, may your pies take
    the prize,
May your Thanksgiving dinner stay off of your thighs!
    —*Author unknown*

You can tell you ate too much for Thanksgiving when you
have to let your bathrobe out.
    —*Jay Leno*

We're having something a little different this year for
Thanksgiving. Instead of a turkey, we're having a swan. You
get more stuffing.
    —*George Carlin*

The Puritans celebrated Thanksgiving day to commemorate
being saved from the Indians. We continue to celebrate it to
commemorate being saved from the Puritans.
    —*Author unknown*

Thanksgiving is an emotional holiday. People travel
thousands of miles to be with people they only see once a
year. And then discover once a year is way too often.
    —*Johnny Carson*

And Lord, we're especially thankful for nuclear power, the cleanest safest energy source there is. Except for solar, which is just a pipe dream. Anyway, we'd like to thank You for the occasional moments of peace and love our family's experienced. Well, not today, You saw what happened! Oh Lord, be honest! Are we the most pathetic family in the universe or what?

> —*Homer Simpson says grace at Thanksgiving dinner, on* The Simpsons

Truth and Lies

A lie can travel halfway around the world while the truth is putting on its shoes.

> —*Mark Twain, attributed*

It is a terrible thing for a man to find out suddenly that all his life he has been speaking nothing but the truth.

> —*Oscar Wilde,* The Importance of Being Earnest

Let us now set forth one of the fundamental truths about marriage: the wife is in charge.

> —*Bill Cosby*

There's one way to find out if a man is honest—ask him. If he says, "Yes," you know he is a crook.
—*Groucho Marx*

There are a terrible lot of lies going around the world, and the worst of it is half of them are true.
—*Winston Churchill*

Truth is the most valuable thing we have. Let us economize it.
—*Mark Twain,* Following the Equator

A little inaccuracy sometimes saves tons of explanation.
—*Saki (H. H. Munro)*

It is perfectly monstrous…the way people go about nowadays saying things against one behind one's back that are absolutely and entirely true.
—*Oscar Wilde,* The Picture of Dorian Gray

In wartime, truth is so precious that she should always be attended by a bodyguard of lies.
—*Winston Churchill*

When in doubt, tell the truth.
   —*Mark Twain,* Following the Equator

You want to be very careful about lying; otherwise you are nearly sure to get caught.
   —*Mark Twain*

That's not a lie. It's a terminological inexactitude.
   —*Alexander Haig*

Let me ask you something: If someone's lying, are their pants really on fire?
   —*Jerry Seinfeld*

One of the most striking differences between a cat and a lie is that a cat has only nine lives.
   —*Mark Twain,* Pudd'nhead Wilson

I told my wife the truth. I told her I was seeing a psychiatrist. Then she told me the truth: that she was seeing a psychiatrist, two plumbers, and a bartender.
   —*Rodney Dangerfield*

I offer my opponents a bargain: if they will stop telling falsehoods about us, I will stop telling the truth about them.
　　—*Adlai Stevenson*

Never tell the truth to people who are not worthy of it.
　　—*Mark Twain*

It is always the best policy to speak the truth—unless, of course, you're an exceptionally good liar.
　　—*Jerome K. Jerome*

If one tells the truth, one is sure, sooner or later, to be found out.
　　—*Oscar Wilde*

You only lie to two people in your life. Your girlfriend and the police.
　　—*Jack Nicholson*

A wise man does not waste so good a commodity as lying for naught.
　　—*Mark Twain,* The Prince and the Pauper

Telling lies is a fault in a boy, an art in a lover, an accomplishment in a bachelor, and second nature in a married man.
> —*Helen Rowland*

There are 869 different forms of lying, but only one of them has been squarely forbidden. Thou shalt not bear false witness against thy neighbor.
> —*Mark Twain,* Following the Equator

A "gaffe" occurs not when a politician lies, but when he tells the truth.
> —*Michael Kinsley*

Women have a hard enough time in this world; telling them the truth would be too cruel.
> —*H. L. Mencken*

The truth is rarely pure and never simple. Modern life would be very tedious if it were either, and modern literature a complete impossibility.
> —*Oscar Wilde,* The Importance of Being Earnest

There are three kinds of lies: lies, damned lies, and statistics.
— *Benjamin Disraeli, attributed*

Get your facts first, and then you can distort them as much as you please.
— *Mark Twain*

The great masses of the people will more easily fall victim to a big lie than to a small one.
— *Adolf Hitler,* Mein Kampf

Lie: A very poor substitute for the truth but the only one discovered up to date.
— *Gideon Wurdz,* The Foolish Dictionary

If you tell the truth, you don't have to remember anything.
— *Mark Twain,* Notebook

Honesty is the best policy, but insanity is a better defense.
— *Steve Landesberg*

Yes, even I am dishonest. Not in many ways, but in some. Forty-one, I think it is.
> —*Mark Twain*

Vice and Virtue

She's the kind of girl who climbed the ladder of success, wrong by wrong.
> —*Mae West, in* I'm No Angel

I can resist everything except temptation.
> —*Oscar Wilde,* Lady Windermere's Fan

Be good and you will be lonesome.
> —*Mark Twain,* Following the Equator

There are no good girls gone wrong—just bad girls found out.
> —*Mae West*

Lead me not into temptation; I can find the way myself.
> —*Rita Mae Brown*

Moderation is a fatal thing....Nothing succeeds like *excess*.
— *Oscar Wilde,* A Woman of No Importance

Vice is its own reward.
— *Quentin Crisp,* The Naked Civil Servant

The censors wouldn't even let me sit on a guy's lap, and I've been on more laps than a table napkin.
— *Mae West*

I used to be Snow White, but I drifted.
— *Mae West*

The more things are forbidden, the more popular they become.
— *Mark Twain,* Notebook

The best way to behave is to misbehave.
— *Mae West*

It's my experience that folks who have no vices have generally very few virtues.
— *Abraham Lincoln*

Vice and Virtue

The only way to get rid of a temptation is to yield to it.
— *Oscar Wilde,* The Picture of Dorian Gray

Between two evils, I always pick the one I never tried before.
— *Mae West, in* Klondike Annie

To err is human—but it feels divine.
— *Mae West*

Pickering: Have you no morals, man?
Doolittle: Can't afford them, Governor.
— *George Bernard Shaw,* Pygmalion

"Goodness, what beautiful diamonds!"
"Goodness had nothing to do with it."
— *Mae West, in* Night After Night

Always do right. This will gratify some people, and astonish the rest.
— *Mark Twain*

I've been things and I've seen places.
— *Mae West, in* I'm No Angel

A man is as good as he has to be, and a woman is as bad as she dares.
> —*Elbert Hubbard*

I'm no angel but I've spread my wings a bit.
> —*Mae West, in* I'm No Angel

Wickedness is a myth invented by good people to account for the curious attractiveness of others.
> —*Oscar Wilde*

Women keep a special corner of their hearts for sins they have never committed.
> —*Cornelia Otis Skinner*

When women go wrong, men go right after them.
> —*Mae West, in* She Done Him Wrong

The only difference between the saint and the sinner is that every saint has a past, and every sinner has a future.
> —*Oscar Wilde,* A Woman of No Importance

It is a sin to believe evil of others, but it is seldom a mistake.
> —*H. L. Mencken*

Nice guys finish last.
> —*Leo Durocher*

I like restraint, if it doesn't go too far.
> —*Mae West*

There are two types of people in this world: good and bad. The good sleep better, but the bad seem to enjoy the waking hours much more.
> —*Woody Allen*

A little sincerity is a dangerous thing, and a great deal of it is absolutely fatal.
> —*Oscar Wilde,* The Critic as Artist

War and Peace

Military intelligence is a contradiction in terms.
> —*Groucho Marx, attributed*

You can no more win a war than you can win an earthquake.
—Jeannette Rankin

When the military man approaches, the world locks up its spoons and packs off its womankind.
—George Bernard Shaw, Man and Superman

In war there is no second prize for the runner-up.
—Omar Bradley

War does not determine who is right—only who is left.
—Bertrand Russell

To jaw-jaw is always better than to war-war.
—Winston Churchill

Men love war because it allows them to look serious. Because it is the one thing that stops women from laughing at them.
—John Fowles

But that was war. Just about all he could find in its favor was that it paid well and liberated children from the pernicious influence of their parents.
— *Joseph Heller,* Catch-22

I believe in compulsory cannibalism. If people were forced to eat what they killed, there would be no more wars.
— *Abbie Hoffman*

You can't say civilization don't advance…for every war they kill you a new way.
— *Will Rogers*

Don't talk to me about naval tradition. It's nothing but rum, sodomy, and the lash.
— *Winston Churchill*

Frankly, I'd like to see the government get out of war altogether and leave the whole field to private industry.
— *Joseph Heller,* Catch-22

I seriously doubt if we will ever have another war. This is probably the very last one.
— *Richard M. Nixon*

The quickest way of ending a war is to lose it.
> —*George Orwell*

We are not retreating. We are advancing in another direction.
> —*Douglas MacArthur, attributed*

The object of war is not to die for your country but to make the other bastard die for his.
> —*George S. Patton*

I don't know what effect these men will have upon the enemy, but, by God, they frighten me.
> —*Duke of Wellington*

Weather

Save a boyfriend for a rainy day. And another, in case it doesn't rain.
> —*Mae West*

Everybody talks about the weather, but nobody does anything about it.
— *Charles Dudley Warner*

Whenever people talk to me about the weather, I always feel quite certain that they mean something else.
— *Oscar Wilde,* The Importance of Being Earnest

Work

It is awfully hard work doing nothing.
— *Oscar Wilde,* The Importance of Being Earnest

I never did a day's work in my life. It was all fun.
— *Thomas A. Edison*

Hard work never killed anybody, but why take the chance?
— *Edgar Bergen*

When you see what some girls marry, you realize how they must hate to work for a living.
— *Helen Rowland*

No laborer in the world is expected to work for room, board, and love—except the housewife.
　　—*Letty Cottin Pogrebin*

Oh, you hate your job? Why didn't you say so? There's a support group for that. It's called EVERYBODY, and they meet at the bar.
　　—*Drew Carey*

I always arrive late at the office, but I make up for it by leaving early.
　　—*Charles Lamb*

All I've ever wanted was an honest week's pay for an honest day's work.
　　—*Steve Martin as Bilko, in* Sgt. Bilko

By working faithfully eight hours a day you may eventually get to be a boss and work twelve hours a day.
　　—*Robert Frost*

Work is the greatest thing in the world, so we should always save some of it for tomorrow.
　　—*Don Herold*

The caterpillar does all the work, but the butterfly gets all the publicity.
— *George Carlin*

My second favorite household chore is ironing. My first being hitting my head on the top bunk bed until I faint.
— *Erma Bombeck*

We live in the age of the over-worked, and the under-educated; the age in which people are so industrious that they become absolutely stupid.
— *Oscar Wilde*

I never work. Work does age you so.
— *Quentin Crisp*

If your house is really a mess and a stranger comes to the door, greet him with, "Who could have done this? We have no enemies."
— *Phyllis Diller*

I like work: it fascinates me. I can sit and look at it for hours.
— *Jerome K. Jerome*, Three Men in a Boat

Hard work is simply the refuge of people who have nothing whatever to do.
> — *Oscar Wilde,* The Remarkable Rocket

If hard work were such a wonderful thing, surely the rich would have kept it all to themselves.
> — *Lane Kirkland*

Work...is so much more fun than fun.
> — *Noël Coward*

Our experts describe you as an appallingly dull fellow, unimaginative, timid, lacking in initiative, spineless, easily dominated, no sense of humor, tedious company and irrepressibly drab and awful. And whereas in most professions these would be considerable drawbacks, in chartered accountancy they are a positive boon.
> — *John Cleese as a guidance counselor,*
> *in* Monty Python's Flying Circus

Work expands so as to fill the time available for its completion.
> — *C. Northcote Parkinson,* Parkinson's Law

The harder I work, the luckier I get.
   — *Samuel Goldwyn*

I never put off till tomorrow what I can possibly do…the day after.
   — *Oscar Wilde*

A man had better wear out than rust out.
   — *Richard Cumberland*

Brains first and then Hard Work.
   — *Eeyore, in* The House at Pooh Corner
   by A. A. Milne

Miscellaneous

Be nice to people on your way up because you'll meet them on your way down.
   — *Wilson Mizner [among others]*

To do nothing is sometimes a good remedy.
   — *Hippocrates*

Those are my principles. If you don't like them, I
have others.
— *Groucho Marx*

All the things I really like are either immoral, illegal,
or fattening.
— *Alexander Woollcott*

Never give a sucker an even break.
— *W. C. Fields [among others]*

The only difference between lawyers and doctors is that
lawyers simply rob you, whereas doctors both rob you and
kill you, too.
— *Anton Chekhov*

When you have nothing to say, say nothing.
— *Charles Caleb Colton*

Anything worth doing is worth doing slowly.
— *Mae West*

Critics are like eunuchs in a harem; they're there every night, they see it done every night, they see how it should be done every night, but they can't do it themselves.
— *Brendan Behan*

Duct tape is like the force. It has a light side, a dark side, and it holds the universe together.
— *Carl Zwanzig*

Everything is funny as long as it is happening to somebody else...
— *Will Rogers*

He who fights and runs away
May live to fight another day;
But he who is in battle slain
Can never rise and fight again.
— *Oliver Goldsmith, attributed*

He who hesitates is last.
— *Mae West*

More than any other time in history mankind faces a crossroads. One path leads to despair and utter

hopelessness; the other, to total extinction. Let us pray that we have the wisdom to choose correctly.
— *Woody Allen*

The secret of life is honesty and fair dealing. If you can fake that, you've got it made.
— *Groucho Marx*

There is only one difference between a madman and me. The madman thinks he is sane. I know I am mad.
— *Salvador Dalí*

I think it would be a good idea.
— *Mahatma Gandhi, when asked what he thought of Western civilization*

What if nothing exists and we're all in somebody's dream? Or, what's worse, what if only that fat guy in the third row exists?
— *Woody Allen,* God: A Comedy in Three Acts

I am free of all prejudices. I hate everyone equally.
— *W. C. Fields*

I don't like myself, I'm crazy about myself.
> —*Mae West*

I am the only person in the world I should like to
know thoroughly.
> —*Oscar Wilde,* Lady Windermere's Fan

If you've got them by the balls, their hearts and minds
will follow.
> —*John Wayne*

It's not the people who are in prison that worry me. It's the
people who aren't.
> —*Arthur Gore*

I am a Bear of Very Little Brain, and long words Bother me.
> —*A. A. Milne,* Winnie-the-Pooh

I've been looking for a girl like you—not you, but a girl
like you.
> —*Groucho Marx*

This suspense is terrible. I hope it will last.
        —*Oscar Wilde,* The Importance of Being Earnest

There's no such thing as bad publicity except your
own obituary.
        —*Brendan Behan*

We can't all be heroes because someone has to sit on the
curb and clap as they go by.
        —*Will Rogers*

Eternity is really long, especially near the end.
        —*Woody Allen*

Owl hasn't exactly got Brain, but he knows Things.
        —*A. A. Milne,* Winnie-the-Pooh

Whenever people agree with me, I always feel I must
be wrong.
        —*Oscar Wilde,* Lady Windermere's Fan

Let Shakespeare do it his way. I'll do it mine. We'll see who comes out better.
> —*Mae West*

I'm astounded by people who want to "know" the universe when it's hard enough to find your way around Chinatown.
> —*Woody Allen*

Please accept my resignation. I don't want to belong to any club that will accept me as a member.
> —*Groucho Marx*

Dancing is a perpendicular expression of a horizontal desire.
> —*George Bernard Shaw*

The biggest sin is sitting on your ass.
> —*Florynce Kennedy*

Take care to get what you like or you will be forced to like what you get.
> —*George Bernard Shaw,* Man and Superman

In matters of grave importance, style, not sincerity is the vital thing.
> —*Oscar Wilde,* The Importance of Being Earnest

When angry, count four; when very angry, swear.
> —*Mark Twain,* Pudd'nhead Wilson

It's hard to be funny when you have to be clean.
> —*Mae West*